MW00679533

THE SEMINARY SEEDS

Father Phil,

thank you for your
service and being such
an inspiration.

Enjoy the book!

Josh
Berry

October 11, 2013

ii

THE SEMINARY SEEDS

BY

FRANK BARRY

www.bookstandpublishing.com

Published by
Bookstand Publishing
Morgan Hill, CA 95037
3898_2

Copyright © 2013 by Frank Barry
All rights reserved. No part of this publication may be reproduced or
transmitted in any form or by any means, electronic or mechanical,
including photocopy, recording, or any information storage and
retrieval system, without permission in writing from the copyright
owner.

ISBN 978-1-61863-523-5

Printed in the United States of America

TABLE OF CONTENTS

PROLOGUE:
ON THE ROAD TO FIND OUT

<u>THE SCENE</u>

Patrick Brennan is racing down the 210 freeway in his classic 57 Chevy away from Los Angeles looking for something but not sure of what. His red hair is blowing in his face, his green eyes intent on the road. He is just days away from his 21st birthday. Cat Stevens is blasting on the CD player, his favorite CD <u>Tea for the Tillerman</u> is playing and the song that seems to exemplify his entire life, "On the Road to Find Out." Patrick left the Catholic seminary after six years and is unsure what to do with his life. He has wandered for months, but something draws him to California. He needs a place of peace and quiet to contemplate the direction he wants to go in life.

He sees the sign: the Huntington Museum and Botanical Gardens. Maybe being surrounded by nature will inspire him. He often walked in the woods that surrounded the seminary in Ohio. He felt closer to God among the trees and flowers even more than when he was in chapel.
He turns down the road leading to the Huntington. He lives in Huntington Beach and maybe there is some cosmic connectivity between the two Huntingtons.

He parks in the lot and follows the signs to the Botanical Gardens. A plaque at the entrance explains that the gardens cover 150 acres with twelve specialized gardens arranged within a park-like landscape of rolling lawns. He considers the list which includes desert, Japanese, and rose gardens. His sister-in-law is Japanese so he heads for the Japanese Garden.

Patrick has always been fascinated with the Japanese culture and the people who revere nature and use gardens as a quiet retreat from the pressures of life. He knows that the three main elements of the Japanese garden are water, rocks, and plants. The seminary for him was that retreat but he discovered that it was not a place to run away from life. It took six years to realize that and for him to leave behind that security blanket and go outside to find his own way. He was here on this road to find out what life had in store for him.

Patrick crosses over the moon bridge and notices the Japanese house in the distance. A sign indicates that he is entering the Zen Court. This seems an appropriate place to think. He finds a bench and begins contemplating his life.

When had the idea formed in his mind that he wanted to be a priest? Was it the influence of his Uncle Leon Loranger a prominent Jesuit in the Catholic Church? Was it from the priests and nuns who saw something in him that suggested that he would make a good priest? What did they see in him? Was it his devotion while serving as an altar boy? Was it his being a studious and disciplined boy? Was it his respect for people demonstrated in his dealings with his peers and adults?

In the eighth grade they gave him an application for the seminary. He was accepted before the end of the school year. He left in September for the Pontifical College Josephinum in Worthington, Ohio. He was following the precepts of the Bible to leave friends and family and follow Him. It was his first time away from home.

For five years he immersed himself in the routine of seminary life- prayer, study, and more prayer. It is in the sixth year that the doubts had begun. Was this the way of life he really wanted? By the end of that year, he knew he had to go out and experience more of the secular life before taking vows. Here he is two thousand miles away in a Japanese garden wondering what he is going to do with the remainder of his life.

He notices a man walking over the moon bridge carrying some kind of plant. As he comes closer, Patrick sees that he is Asian dressed in old coveralls and wearing work gloves. His hair is grey and thick, his face weathered. Their eyes meet for just a few seconds. The man turns toward Patrick and approaches him.

OLD MAN: Young man, you seem lost in thought.

PATRICK: Good morning. (Patrick doesn't know if he wants to talk to anyone right now.)

OLD MAN: This is a good place to think. My name is Yoshiro. You can call me Yoshi. (He bows and then extends his hand which Patrick shakes.)

PATRICK: What is that you are carrying?

viii

YOSHI: This is a bonsai tree. I am heading to the Bonsai Garden. Would you like to join me?

(Patrick hesitates.)

YOSHI: Don't worry. I will not ply you with questions. If you prefer silence, I will respect that.
(Patrick follows the man and thinks about the other Man he had been following for six years.)

PATRICK: Do you work here at the garden? (Patrick decides he does need some conversation.)

YOSHI: Yes, but I do not call it work. For me it is a labor of joy. I find that nature is a wonderful place to exist in and make my life. Take this bonsai tree, for example, it is intentionally dwarfed by pruning and despite its stature, brings joy to those who nurture it.

PATRICK: I guess there is a lesson there for all of us. Our lives could all use a little pruning in certain areas.

YOSHI: Is that what you are doing here today, thinking about your life?'

(Yoshiro looks into Patrick's eyes. Patrick feels a sudden warmth towards this man. He seems interested in him as a person. They sit on a bench beside a small Koi pond. Patrick can see the fish swimming around rapidly probably aware of their presence.)

PATRICK: Yes, I have just closed one chapter of my life and am trying to decide what to do now.

YOSHI: You sound sad about this closing. Was it painful? (Yoshi sets the bonsai down between them on the bench.)

PATRICK: Not so much painful but I am fearful for the future. I don't feel that I am prepared for anything that involves making a living.

YOSHI: What have you done so far in life? (The man turns to Patrick and looks again into his eyes. The man seems to be looking deeper. Patrick feels comfortable opening up to him.)

PATRICK: I just left a seminary after six years. (Patrick lowers his eyes and head.)

YOSHI: Why do you say this with such regret?

PATRICK: Because I feel that I didn't learn anything that will help me in my life.

YOSHI: Young man...

PATRICK: Patrick.

YOSHI: Patrick, I think you need to examine the experience and you will find that you have many lessons that you learned that can be applied to your life. I would be honored to explore that with you as I have had a similar experience. (The man stands and hands the bonsai to Patrick.) Take this as a token of my sincerity. I am unable to spend more time today but come back tomorrow. (Yoshiro bows and walks away. Patrick looks intently at the bonsai.)

PATRICK: Thank you! (He yells, but Yoshi keeps on walking.)

As he drives out of the Huntington Gardens, Patrick is thinking that maybe this is the road on which he will find out where his life will lead.

Seed 1. A Vocation is a Calling-Follow Your Heart

"I think most of us are looking for a calling, not a job. Most of us, like the assembly line worker have jobs that are too small for our spirit. Jobs are not big enough for people."
Studs Terkel, "Working"

THE SCENE

The next day Patrick finds Yoshi kneeling on the ground not far from the bench where they had talked the day before. Patrick stands quietly and watches the man work, his hands forming mounds of earth around the flowers. He moves quickly but gently. After a few minutes, the silence is broken.

YOSHI: Good morning, Patrick. I will continue to work while we talk. How are you feeling today?

PATRICK: I feel good. I think that having someone to bounce ideas off of will help me.

YOSHI: (looks up) Yes, it is good to share thoughts with others who can maybe give you a different perspective. Yesterday, you said that you felt that the six years in the seminary did not give you much on which to base your life or words to that effect. Why do you think that?

PATRICK (thinks for a few minutes before answering) I remember receiving the letter from the diocese that I had been accepted and falling to my knees and giving thanks. I felt that I had truly been called…my vocation or calling was to the priesthood. In my heart, I felt such joy even at that age of fourteen. The lines of the Bible came to mind, 'Many are called but few are chosen.' I was to be one of the chosen few.

YOSHI: What lead you to make a decision at that age to follow the religious life?
(That was a question that Patrick had asked himself many times.)

PATRICK: The Catholic Church had played a big role in my life. Besides having family who were nuns and priests, I had always felt comfortable in the church. Being an altar boy brought me closer to the rituals than most people. I often saw myself as the priest lifting the cup and changing the water into wine. I saw how the priests and nuns dedicated themselves to serving others.

YOSHI: So it was the service that attracted you, not just the trappings of the church but the actual ministry. Correct? (Yoshi stands and faces Patrick.)

PATRICK: Yes, now that I think about it, it was all the duties of the priest that attracted me: administering the sacraments, being involved with the youth at CYO (Catholic Youth Organization) dances, community events such as festivals and bingo. The priest was among the people doing the Lord's work. It was that sense of community that I liked.
(Yoshi gestures to Patrick to join him on a bench.)

YOSHI: Time for a short break. It sounds to me that your heart is telling you that your life must have that sense of service. What was it about that service you felt affected you in the seminary?

PATRICK: (sits next to Yoshi.) I know that in the seminary I felt a peace, a calm that I had only experienced in church on Sundays but there it was constant. Even in the refectory eating with a hundred other boys, there was a sense of peace. In my heart, I knew that this was the place I wanted to be and the life I was called for.

YOSHI: You were following your heart. (Toshiro says softly.) Let me tell you a story. There was a farmer who lived in the flatlands of the Midwest. Due to the climate and the economy, uncertainty and change were the only constants. The survival of the farm depended on his ability to successfully face the changes and avoid disasters.

This day the sky was very strange. The farmer noticed the restlessness of the animals and heard the sound of their cries.

Because he was an alert, he recognized this behavior as an advance sign of an impending storm. If he hadn't noticed this warning signs, the storm could have come upon him suddenly and unexpectedly. The frightened animals would have scattered across the plain. The farm and possibly the lives of his family would have been lost.

But the farmer had his eyes and ears open. He recognized the signs and responded quickly. He lead his animals to a secure area, he tied down his equipment, and led his family to the storm shelter. A tornado hit just a short time later. Watching and listening for signs of change allowed him to save his family and farm.

Now what lesson do you get from this story?

PATRICK: I need to watch and listen for signs.

YOSHI: Yes, but signs of what? Think back to the seminary, what signs were there that made the change in your heart and mind?
(Patrick sits quietly for a few minutes thinking about the past.)

PATRICK: I was happiest when I was interacting with other people. I didn't like the night silence-those hours from 7:30 at night until after breakfast when we couldn't speak. I understood the need for the discipline, but it was very difficult to not communicate during this time. I was caught talking once and was ordered to kneel out which was a punishment. I had to kneel in front of the Prefect's door and hope he would not find me there because the humiliation of having broken the night silence rule was worse than the pain in my knees.

YOSHI: Could this have been a sign that this life was not for you?

PATRICK: It was more than just that. I found myself wanting to explore beyond the walls. We were not allowed outside of the seminary grounds except once a month-a five mile walk to Westerville, the nearest town. Even this I rebelled at and hitched a ride leading to a punishment that kept me from the next hike. It was not a pleasant time sitting alone when all the other students were outside the walls. My heart just wasn't in it anymore. I began to rethink my motivation for being there and if I truly wanted to dedicate my life to Christ.

YOSHI: You must remember that you were a teenager at a time in life when one is trying to make sense of the world and find one's place in it.

PATRICK: It was the world that lured me away. (Blurts out with some emotion.)

YOSHI: I sense that it was not the religious world drawing you away.

PATRICK: You're right. During the summers when I was home with my family, I no longer felt close to my family. My nine month absence seemed to distance us. My brothers and sisters were all caught up in fun things like television and games. They would talk about TV shows that I had not knowledge of or excitement about. Even the music was foreign to me. Coming home was like landing on another planet. It was a different world which I no longer felt a part of.

YOSHI: Christ did ask his disciples to leave family behind and follow him. You were making a sacrifice to pursue your vocation.

PATRICK: I understood the need, but I began to question the want. Was it what I wanted? I felt that the call to the priestly life was fading in my heart. I had to follow a new path. The passion for the vocation was gone. There was a fire at the beginning, but now it was being extinguished. I faced up to it and left the seminary.

YOSHI: Patrick, your passion was now being directed to a different area of life. Your heart told you to take another path. I felt that passion when you talked about dedicating your life to helping others. That may be the biggest and best lesson you learned that the passion may change which is especially true when one is young and exploring various paths in life. Take heart that you learned the lesson and now it is time to move on.

PATRICK: You are right, Yoshi.

YOSHI: Let's explore more tomorrow, Patrick. You are just touching the tip of what you can draw from your past experiences, but it is important to understand that what you have learned will guide your future.

Final Thought:
"You can't pry the petals of a flower open, but you can provide the flower with healthy soil and plenty of sunlight and water. Then, when the petals do blossom, they will enfold in just the right way and time, and the flower will be an expression of beauty and grace."
Alan H. Cohen

Yoshi's Yardsticks for Success:
Make your passion your profession! What is your passion? Write it
down here.

_____

_____

_____

Listen for signs that may point your life in the direction of your dreams.
What are your dreams? Write them here.

_____

_____

_____

Are there any signs that you have picked up on? Write them here.

_____

_____

_____

Thought for the Day:
*"There is so much in the world for us all if we only have the eyes to see
it, and the heart to love it, and the hand to gather it to ourselves...."*
Lucy Maud Montgomery (1874-1942)

6

Seed 2. A Regimen Pays Dividends: Set Goals

<u>THE SCENE</u>

The next day Patrick finds Yoshi in the rose garden. Immediately Patrick thinks of the saying that life is no bed of roses and is smiling when he sees Yoshi.

YOSHI: Patrick, you find something amusing?

PATRICK: I was just thinking about that old saying about life being no bed of roses.

YOSHI: In reality, life is like a bed of roses. (Yoshi bends a rose towards Patrick.) Though there may be some thorns, I like to think of them as challenges, there is still beauty. Beauty is indeed in the eye of the beholder but more importantly, our minds eye makes it so. So it is with life. You have talked about the challenges of the seminary, but what was it you found beautiful?
(Patrick sits on the grass and thinks before answering.)

PATRICK: One of the aspects of seminary life was the daily regimen. Our day was pretty much laid out for us.

YOSHI: What was a typical day like for you, Patrick?

PATRICK: The deacon assigned to our dorm turned on the lights at 5:00 a.m. every morning. We had an hour to clean up, dress, and make our beds. The night silence was still in effect so all of this was done quietly and efficiently. There was no distraction from out tasks. The first bell was at 5:50 when we all headed down to the chapel.

There was morning meditation followed by Mass. There were actually eleven masses going on at once-ten on the side altars and one on the main altar. The priests on the faculty all had to say daily mass. Then breakfast was at 7:00 and when we filed out of the refectory, night silence was over, and it was like an explosion-hundreds of boys bursting into conversation. Classes ran all morning with a short break in the middle and lunch at 11:30. There was silence at lunch as an inspirational book was read. After lunch was walking time and then afternoon classes. Dinner was at 5:00 followed by two hours of study hall, the rosary which began the night silence, and then bed at 9:00 p.m."

YOSHI: That was quite a full schedule. Was it the same routine every day? (Yoshi stops pruning the roses and concentrates on Patrick.)

PATRICK: Wednesday afternoons were for sports activities which included everything from basketball and baseball to ice skating in the winter. The half day was made up with Saturday morning classes and more sports in that afternoon. Sundays we attended two masses a high mass and a low mass. That was the day to study and prepare for the week ahead.

YOSHI: By the tone of your voice, it seems that you didn't mind that schedule.

PATRICK: Not at all. I liked knowing what was coming next and when. You didn't have to think about what to do at any hour. It was only on Sunday afternoons that you had a choice of activities-study or play. The regimen suited me fine.

YOSHI: The question now, Patrick, is how do you take that experience and use it to make a better life for yourself?

PATRICK: I admit that I have been lazy and wandering aimlessly for the past months. I really had no agenda to follow. Without the direction of the seminary regimen, I was lost.

YOSHI: You have not taken command of your own destiny, right?

PATRICK: Right! I have been going with the flow rather than directing the flow of my life.

8

YOSHI: So what can you do to change that?

PATRICK: First, I have to decide on a direction for my life. Once I do that, I can plan out the daily activities which will take me there.

YOSHI: What you need, Patrick, are goals. Those are what will give you the direction you need. Then you can set up a regimen that will allow you to achieve your goals. Does that make sense?

PATRICK: That would be the smart thing to do.

YOSHI: Speaking of smart, do you know the SMART criteria for goal setting, Patrick?

PATRICK: No, but I would like to hear them.

YOSHI: I will write them out for you with an explanation. Do you have a pad of paper and a pen?

PATRICK: I have one in the car. Let me go get it.
(A few minutes later Patrick returns with paper and pen, and Yoshi draws out the SMART criteria for goal setting.)
The "S" stands for **"Specific"**- a specific goal has a much better chance of being accomplished than a general goal. To set a specific goal you must answer the six "W" questions:

Who:	Who is involved in the goal?
What:	What do I want to accomplish?
Where:	Identify a location.
When:	Establish a time frame.
Which:	Identify requirements and obstacles.
Why:	Specific reasons, purpose or benefits of accomplishing the goal.

YOSHI: Patrick, if you were to set a goal of buying a new car, what kind would you buy?

PATRICK: I guess, an economical one.

YOSHI: Part of being specific is decision making-decide which car. Name one that you would like to own.

PATRICK: A hybrid."

YOSHI: What model?

PATRICK: A Ford Fusion.

YOSHI: What color?

PATRICK: Blue

YOSHI: How many doors?

PATRICK: A two door.

YOSHI: A hardtop or convertible?

PATRICK: Convertible so I can enjoy the beautiful California weather while driving.

YOSHI: What extras?

PATRICK: A great sound system, a GPS system, video in the rear.

YOSHI: Are you getting the idea, Patrick? You must get that specific so your mind can see the exact car you want. Another way to help you achieve that goal is to get a picture of the car and put it some place where you can see it everyday such as the refrigerator or on the visor of your current car. In sight, in mind!

PATRICK: Yoshi, I get it. I have to connect my goal to details, specifics. There is no grey area here.

YOSHI: That's exactly right. Now let's talk about the "M."

The 'M' stands for **Measurable.** You must set concrete criteria for measuring progress toward the attainment of each goal you set. There is a saying that what gets measured, gets done. When you measure your progress, you stay on track, reach your target dates, and experience the exhilaration of achievement that spurs you on to continued effort required to reach your goal. Ask the questions: how much or how many or how will I know when it is accomplished?

Let's use you car goal as an example. What could you measure that would keep you on track for getting the car you want?
(Patrick thinks for a moment.)

PATRICK: I would have to save money for a down payment. I could track my savings.

YOSHI: That's good, Patrick. You would already know how much to save because you were specific in the car you wanted and know its price. Say your research showed that you'd need $3,000 to cover down payment, licenses, fees, and insurance. We will discuss timeline later but let's say that you have set the goal that you will purchase the car in 2 ½ years or 30 months. How much per month will you have to save to reach your goal?

PATRICK: Yoshi, I was terrible at math but this one I can solve-$100 a month.

YOSHI: Correct, so at the end of every month you look at your plan and can tell if you met your measurable goal of saving $100 a month.

PATRICK: Wow, I can't wait to get started.

YOSHI: Good, Patrick, you are getting excited about what goal setting can do for your life. You can do it if you put your mind to it. You proved that in the seminary. Now let's talk about the "A."

The 'A' stands for **Attainable.** Patrick, you can attain most any goal you set when you plan your steps wisely (the specifics we talked about) and establish a time frame that allows you to carry out those steps. When you set your goals, you are building your self-image by giving yourself a purpose. You must see yourself as worthy of these goals, and develop the traits and personality that allow you to possess them.

PATRICK: Phew, Yoshi, there are a lot of things involved in this goal setting. I am getting the idea that it is more than just a list of things to do.

YOSHI: You are right. The exercise of goal setting is also about attitudes specifically PMA-Positive Mental Attitude. It is also about ability, your being able to achieve what you want in life. It also takes some skills- like time management, organization, and problem solving. Do you have what it takes to get that car of yours?

PATRICK: Inside of me yes, but in reality not the external things I need to do. Not yet.

YOSHI: Let's talk about reality because the "R" stands for **R**ealistic-a goal must represent an objective toward which you are both <u>willing</u> and <u>able</u> to work. Are you willing to do what it takes to reach that goal, Patrick?

PATRICK: I know that I can achieve what I put my mind to. I am willing, yes.

YOSHI: Are you able to work toward the goal?

PATRICK: Yoshi, the word "work" to me has a negative connotation. I would rather make it a fun exercise somehow.

YOSHI: You can do that, Patrick. It has to do with your own motivation. A higher goal is frequently easier to reach than a lower one because a low goal exerts low motivational force. I would set the highest goal possible to challenge yourself because the reward will be greater too. Your goal is probably realistic if you truly <u>believe </u>that it can be accomplished. A good way to determine if your goal is realistic is to determine if you have accomplished anything similar in the past. Is there something you achieved in the past that would indicate you can reach your current goals?
(Patrick thinks for a few moments.)

PATRICK: Yes, I had a goal as a teen to buy an encyclopedia and I set a deadline and a savings plan. I reached it ahead of time, actually.

YOSHI: I am glad you mentioned a deadline because the "T" in "SMART" means **Timely** or **Time-bound** because someday won't work. A goal should be grounded within a time frame. When you set a date, you've set your unconscious mind into motion to begin working on the goal. With no time frame tied to it there's no sense of urgency. If you want to lose 10 pounds, when do you want to lose it by? If you say by September 1, you've got a time frame which can motivate you. You set a 30 month savings plan for your car so you already know about timelines. One final piece of advice, write down your goals. There is something about putting the words on paper that instill them in your mind.

PATRICK: I am going to work on my goals. You have inspired me.

YOSHI: Go for it, Patrick. See you soon.

Yoshi's Yardsticks for Success:
What one major goal do you want to achieve in the next year?

___

Apply the SMART criteria to your goal.

S_____
_____

M_____
_____

A_____
_____

R_____
_____

T_____
_____

Thought for the Day:

Seneca said, "If a man knows not what harbor he seeks, any wind is the right wind."

Seed 3. The Balancing Act: Work, Prayer, Recreation

<u>THE SCENE</u>

Patrick doesn't see Yoshi again for a few days. He runs to him waving a sheaf of papers.

PATRICK: Yoshi, I have my goals all written out. I am excited.

YOSHI: No wonder I haven't seen you for a while. You have been busy.

PATRICK: Yes, but a good busy. I feel I have the direction I need now and a guide to achieve my goals.

YOSHI: Patrick, one thing that will help you is to manage your time. You need to balance out your life so that you give the appropriate time to each role in your life. How were you able to accomplish so much in your day in the seminary?

PATRICK: Our day was planned carefully. There was a time for each activity-studying, prayer, eating, sleeping, and even recreation.

YOSHI: Did you ever get burned out say from studying?

PATRICK: No, I don't ever recall that though at times I felt there was so much to study as we had six courses every semester. Now that I think of it, there was never an over exertion on one aspect of our lives there. There seemed to be an equal amount of time for our every activity.

YOSHI: That is something you can apply at this time of your life. I meet people here whom I can tell are burned out. They look tired and sometimes I find them just sitting on a bench hunched over like the weight of the world is on their shoulders. They come here for a short rest and then return to their own rat race. (Yoshi looks to a bench in the distance.)

PATRICK: I suspect that nothing will change unless they take charge of their lives.

YOSHI: You are right, Patrick, only they can get off the treadmill but many times just adding some balance to their lives can help. Did you ever hear that Irish prayer about taking time?

PATRICK: I do remember parts of it. Do you know it?

YOSHI:

> *Take time to work,*
> *It is the price of success.*
> *Take time to think,*
> *It is the source of power.*
> *Take time to play,*
> *It is the secret of perpetual youth.*
> *Take time to read,*
> *It is the foundation of wisdom.*
> *Take time to be friendly,*
> *It is the road to happiness.*
> *Take time to love and be loved,*
> *It is the privilege of the gods.*
> *Take time to share,*
> *Life is too short to be selfish.*
> *Take time to laugh,*
> *Laughter is the music of the soul.*

PATRICK: My ancestors surely had the wisdom for the ages. I remember my grandmother saying something similar to me when I was young.

YOSHI: There are reasons, Patrick, why these words have lasted the test of time.

16

Think about each piece of advice and let's see how you can apply it to your life. Notice words "work" and "success" are together.

PATRICK: I once heard someone say that the only place success comes before work is in the dictionary. I really believe that you have to work hard to succeed. I remember my father working long hours at the textile mill to take care of our family's needs. He moved up into a supervisory position. He left me with a great work ethic.

YOSHI: You know, Patrick, I talk to a lot of people here in the gardens and I sense that many people feel that they will have success handed to them on a silver platter. It's almost as if they feel it is their right, but we both know that nothing comes easy in life. I too had to work hard to be where I am today. Coming from Japan years ago, I knew I would have to learn English and to be a gardener, learn all I could about plants and soil but the rewards are great.

PATRICK: I know that to reach my goals, I am going to have to work at them.

YOSHI: I also like the other idea in the prayer that we need to take time to think that it is the source of power. What kind of power do you think it is referring to, Patrick?

PATRICK: The power of thought has to do with the use of our brains-using the God-given talents we all have.

YOSHI: I believe it is more than that. It is taking time to meditate and pray. It may be just taking a few minutes to stop and focus rather than be in constant activity which most people are. The power comes from inside ourselves and we can discover that power through prayer. What was your experience in the seminary?

PATRICK: Right before mass in the morning, we had fifteen minutes of meditation. We would take a line out of a book such as the Bible and meditate on each word's meaning.

YOSHI: Can you give me an example, Patrick?

PATRICK: Yes, here's one that you can identify with. 'What so ye shall reap, ye shall sow.'

YOSHI: (laughing) I've done a lot of sowing here.

PATRICK: And look what you have reaped, acres of beautiful plants and flowers for people to enjoy. What our meditation did was take the main words "reap" and "sow" and think about their meanings both in the literal sense and the spiritual sense. In the seminary we were sowing a lot of seeds that would eventually sprout for us later in life.

YOSHI: But Patrick, you were also sowing seeds in the seminary by study and prayer that were paying off for you at that time.

PATRICK: You are right. The time we spent in study paid off big dividends by helping us grow intellectually. The time in prayer helped us grow spiritually. The time in recreation helped us grow physically.

YOSHI: Don't you think this same investment now can help you grow in all those areas again?

PATRICK: Absolutely! I really can't see myself not continuing to grow.

YOSHI: I read a great quote, Patrick. 'When you are green, you grow; when you are ripe, you rot.' I can't see you rotting away.

PATRICK: No, Yoshi. You are right. I want to grow as a person.

YOSHI: Remember that the prayer also says to take time to play as it is the secret to perpetual youth.

PATRICK: You know I used to hate taking part in various sports in the seminary. It was mandatory that we participate. I wanted to be in my room reading rather than on a cold, wet football field or in sub-zero weather ice skating. Now looking back, I am glad I did participate because I have an appreciation for sports and the athletes. It helped me develop physically and cleared my mind so that I could handle the rigorous class requirements.

YOSHI: We often don't appreciate our experiences until we can look back and see how they have affected our lives. You already mentioned you liked to read and as the prayer says, it is the foundation of wisdom. What did you read in the seminary?

PATRICK: I was exposed to great works of literature, many of them we read in the original language such as Caesar's Gallic Wars in Latin, Wilhelm Tell in German, The Summa Theologica by St. Thomas Aquainas.

YOSHI: Patrick, that was quite an accomplishment. So you know Latin and German? Latin is very valuable as it is the basis of the romance languages so you can learn those very easily.

PATRICK: I never thought about it that way but having that foundation could be very important in a future career. I did struggle, though, with the grammar of both languages but I was able to plow through it.

YOSHI: I am sure it wasn't easy but knowledge of other languages can be very influential in your life choices. I know my knowledge of Japanese and English plus my skills with various plants and flowers where instrumental in my being able to work in the Japanese garden.

PATRICK: I need to explore some careers where multiple languages will be helpful.

YOSHI: That goes along with the next admonition about taking time to be friendly as it is the road to happiness. People skills are an important component to success. Combined with your knowledge of languages, it could really lead you on a path that will bring you not only happiness, but self-fulfillment.

PATRICK: Being friendly is a good way for me to meet new people. I know that there is a philosophy that states what you put out will return. I always believed that what I extend to others will come back to me.

YOSHI: When I gave you that banzai tree, Patrick, I was not looking for anything in return but I did receive something and it was the happiness you expressed by receiving that gift. I heard a very touching story that exemplifies this concept of happiness and friendliness.

YOSHI: (sits on the bench and relates the following story)

There was a young boy, we will call him Ben, whose family moved to a new city. Ben was very nervous about going to a new school. He had made many friends at his old school and leaving them made him very sad. In the new school he felt lonely. No one made an effort to extend any friendship to him. The Friday of the first week as he was walking home, he dropped all his books and fell to the ground and cried. He felt a hand on his shoulder and he looked up and saw a boy who introduced himself as Jerry who helped Ben pick up his books. Jerry walked Ben home and they became friends.

Sixty years later, Ben was dying in a hospice and called Jerry to his bedside and made this confession. On that day sixty years ago when Ben dropped his books, he had decided to kill himself when he got home but Jerry's intervention had saved Ben's life. Jerry's act of kindness had changed the course of Ben's life.

(Patrick is unable to speak for a few minutes.)

PATRICK: That really makes me think about how a small act can generate big consequences in people's lives. We never really know what is going on in someone's life or what turmoil they may be going through.

YOSHI: True, that is why it is important to extend that hand of friendship because what we are really talking about is taking the time to love. Though the prayer says it is the privilege of the gods, I think it would be more correct to say it is the privilege of man to be godlike.

PATRICK: I also like the admonition about sharing. It is paired with the idea that life is too short to be selfish. There is a lot in that stanza to contemplate.

YOSHI: There is a philosophy, Patrick, that states what we share multiplies, what we withhold diminishes. I know in my own life, I have seen the results of sharing and how it has had an almost domino effect. Years ago, a restaurant owner named Frank Garcia began a non-profit organization called We Give Thanks in Anaheim.

PATRICK: That's where Disneyland is.

YOSHI: Yes, another example of a man sharing his vision and the multiple effects. Frank started out feeding a few hundred people on Thanksgiving Day in the parking lot of his restaurant. He did not put any restrictions on who could come to the dinner. Anyone who was hungry and wanted a meal got one. Now he feeds over 15,000 people on that day. His generosity has multiplied because so many people joined this event including major corporations. I had the opportunity to meet Frank a few years ago and can tell you this man has a heart as big as Texas where he was raised.

PATRICK: That is certainly an example of how one person's sharing can affect so many lives. There are so many examples of one can make a difference and change the world. Ghandi and Martin Luther King come to mind.

YOSHI: You know, I think we forget that though these people are famous, there are so many people who everyday share their talents and skills to make a difference in the world. You are talking about becoming a teacher which is one profession that makes a difference every day.

PATRICK: This is all so serious. Maybe that is why the prayer ended with laughter as music of the soul. It wanted to remind us not to take life so seriously that we cannot find humor in it or just find enjoyment.

YOSHI: If you have read the latest studies, you will discover that laughter is not only good for the soul but for one's health. Are you familiar with Norman Cousins?

PATRICK: No.

YOSHI: Cousins did research at UCLA on the biochemistry of human emotions, which he believed were the key to human beings' success in fighting illness. Even as he battled heart disease, he put this belief in practice by taking massive doses of Vitamin C, and he trained himself to laugh. He wrote a 1980 memoir, *Human Options: An Autobiographical Notebook*. His struggle with reactive arthritis is detailed in the book and movie *Anatomy of an Illness*. Cousins developed a recovery program incorporating megadoses of Vitamin C, along with a positive attitude, love, faith, hope, and laughter induced by Marx Brothers films. He discovered that ten minutes of genuine belly laughter had an anesthetic effect and would give him at least two hours of pain-free sleep.

When the pain-killing effect of the laughter wore off, he would switch on the motion picture projector again and not infrequently, it would lead to another pain-free interval.

Cousins died of heart failure on November 30, 1990, in L.A. He lived 10 years after his first heart attack, 16 years after his collagen illness, and 36 years after his doctors first diagnosed his heart disease.

PATRICK: I will put his books on my reading list. I have not done too much laughing lately so maybe I need to take in a Marx Brothers film.

YOSHI: That will be good both for your soul and your health. Speaking of taking time, I think I have taken enough of your time today. Let's get together soon.

PATRICK: I feel that is time worthwhile that I spend with you. I learn so much and it is so good to have someone to share ideas and stories with. See you soon.

Yoshi's Yardsticks for Success:
Set a goal in each area by taking time to:
Work: do one thing this week to be successful in your work:

Think: do one thing this week to use the power of thought:

Play: do something this week that is playful:

Read: pick up a book this week that will increase your knowledge in a subject that could positively affect your life.

Friendly: extend the hand of friendship to someone this week.

Love: express your love this week to someone important in your life.

Share: share something that you have with someone who doesn't have it.

Laugh: pick up a comic film or read some jokes and laugh.

Thought for the Day:
"Happiness is a perfume you cannot pour on others without getting a few drops on yourself."
Ralph Waldo Emerson (1803-1882)

Seed 4. Save Your Knees by Obedience

A few days later Patrick finds Yoshi kneeling in front of the Koi pond.

YOSHI: Good day, Patrick, why don't you join me here on the ground and we can continue your examination of your past.

PATRICK: Thanks, but I will sit, not kneel.

YOSHI: Is there a problem with kneeling?

PATRICK: My memories of that are not too pleasant.

YOSHI: Explain please.

PATRICK: As you can imagine, we spent a lot of time on our knees. This is to be expected when you are praying, but there were other times when we knelt and that was for punishment.

YOSHI: (laughs) Were all those hours in chapel torture for you?

PATRICK: No, though the kneelers were made of wood and very hard on the knees, I didn't find that difficult. Over the months we actually built up calluses which became a cushion of sorts. I am referring to the practice of "kneeling out" as it was called in the seminary.

YOSHI: I've heard the term "kneeling down," but never "kneeling out."

PATRICK: This happened during night silence time which was from seven-thirty in the evening until seven-thirty in the morning. If we broke the silence in any way, we would have to kneel on the floor for about fifteen minutes.

YOSHI: Was it only by talking you broke the silence?

PATRICK: Actually it was by any form of communication. You could signal another student or pass a note or throw a wad of paper. If the deacon caught you, he would call you out and have you kneel. Some deacons were very strict but others let you get away with some things. We were teens after all and though dedicated to the spiritual life, still liked to play.

YOSHI: I take it you had to kneel out on occasion?

PATRICK: Yes, one night in the dorm I got caught whispering to the student in the bed next to me, but it was not just the kneeling out that was bad.

YOSHI: I can imagine you were somewhat embarrassed.

PATRICK: The worst part was that I had to kneel out in front of the Prefect's door. He was a priest who had taken me under his wing. I was ashamed that I had somehow betrayed his trust. He was not in his room so that thirty minutes I sweated out his coming to his room and finding me kneeling there.

YOSHI: Did he catch you?

PATRICK: Yes, just minutes before my time was up, he came to his room and asked me what I had done to deserve the punishment. I told him that I had broken the night silence. His question about what I had learned made me admit that if I broke the rules, I had to pay the price. He told me to go back to bed.

YOSHI: So this transgression resulted in a learning experience for you. Did you break the night silence again?

PATRICK: No. I towed the line after that.

YOSHI: I think it was a good thing you got caught and had to kneel out.

PATRICK: Why?

YOSHI: Because early in life you learned a valuable lesson, every action has a consequence of some kind attached to it. If you break a rule, you have to make amends. Some people do not find that out until later in life and by then, the consequences can be dire such as going to prison.

PATRICK: I never thought of it like that.

YOSHI: Did you study physics in the seminary?

PATRICK: Yes, though I didn't do well in the course.

YOSHI: Then you know one of the principles of physics is that for every action is there an equal reaction. In the realm of morality, it is true that our actions cause reactions that can resonate with others.

PATRICK: My knees certainly resonated by my breaking the night silence rule.

YOSHI: It can be tragic in some cases. Let me give you a good example. Teens love to party and part of that is doing adult things. They are in a hurry to grow up and can't wait until 21 to drink so they have a party in somebody's house where there is a lot of alcohol. One boy drives home drunk and hits a car killing the driver and causing a little girl who was in the passenger seat to be paralyzed for the rest of her life. His actions affected and changed the lives of others. He has to pay the consequences.

PATRICK: There is another element here, Yoshi. We need to think of the consequences prior to the action. In the above case, the boy should have considered what the possible outcomes would be of his drinking and driving.

YOSHI: Yes, but rarely do we stop and think before we do something like drink. There was a television program called "Truth or Consequences" and the premise was that if a contestant didn't answer a question correctly, he/she would have to pay the consequences which were usually performing some stunt. Let's play a version of that. Are you game?

PATRICK: Okay, Yoshi, as long as it's not Madonna's "Truth or Dare".

YOSHI: (laughs) No, there will be no dares. I will give you an action and you tell me what the consequence would be. Ready?

PATRICK: Go for it.

YOSHI: Not fastening your seatbelt while driving.

PATRICK: Flying through the windshield in a serious accident. I click it or I get a ticket. That's the law.

YOSHI: Eating a lot of fast food.

PATRICK: I saw the documentary *Supersize Me* so I know the consequences of eating too much fast food. I would gain weight and join the ranks of the obese.

YOSHI: Being a couch potato.

PATRICK: I learned in the seminary to stay active and keep the body in shape. I work out three to four times a week at the gym. I know how bad I feel when I skip my workouts.

YOSHI: Having unprotected sex.

PATRICK: Yo, Yoshi. You are getting serious here. I live in the age of AIDS so I am not going to jeopardize my life in that way. I read recently that STDs-sexually transmitted diseases are on the rise so you can be sure that I will use protection.

YOSHI: Using drugs.

PATRICK: I was never around drugs thanks to the clean seminary life, but I have seen the results of addiction. I have family members who were alcoholics and one who was addicted to cocaine. They lost everything including relationships and homes. If there is such a thing as learning from someone else's mistakes, then I have plenty of examples.

28

YOSHI: I think you have the idea by now that your future depends on the decisions that you make and for every decision, there is an outcome or consequence. So as you are examining your past life, use the lessons to serve you well in the future. The consequences would be a lot worse than having to kneel. They could kill.

PATRICK: Thanks, Yoshi. You gave me a lot to think about. I think the word "truth" is important in the phrase "truth or consequences" because when it comes right down to it, I have to be truthful with myself about my habits and what they could lead to.
Every time I get into my car, I automatically put on my seatbelt. It has almost become a reflex action, but it is good to think about the consequences. I have to hit the road.

YOSHI: Stay safe, Patrick.

PATRICK: You too, Yoshi. See you again soon.

Yoshi's Yardsticks for Success:
Set a goal in each of the following areas of your life that will help you avoid negative consequences. Phrase it in a positive way beginning with "I will + an action word...."

Health:_____
_____

Eating:_____
_____

Driving_____
_____

Communication:_____
_____

Relationships:_____
_____

Thought for the Day:

On the television show, *Truth or Consequences*, host Bob Barker's signoff ended with the phrase, "Hoping all your consequences are happy ones."

Seed 5. Consideration for Others

Patrick finds Yoshi working in the Zen Garden and sits quietly while the man tends to the landscape. After about twenty minutes, Yoshi acknowledges him.

YOSHI: Patrick, you are a special type of person. Most people just bust in without any consideration but you sat there quietly allowing me to work uninterrupted. What do you say about that?

PATRICK: One thing the seminary focused on was consideration for others. As aspiring priests, we knew that our lives would be dedicated to helping people. We had to be people-focused which included being considerate.

YOSHI: That is some quality to have and unfortunately I don't see a lot of consideration for others today. For example, a simple act of holding the door open for someone coming behind you is being considerate, but many times people will just let a door slam in someone's face.

PATRICK: Yoshi, I experienced something a few weeks ago that made me stop and think. I usually look behind me when coming out of a door and I noticed a woman about to exit so I held the door for her. She thanked me and said: 'You had a good upbringing, young man.'
It made me realize that many of our social interactions have a lot to do with influences in our lives. Not only did the seminary influence me but so did my parents who taught me to be considerate of others.

YOSHI: That is a good point, Patrick, many times we imitate the behavior of those around us which can be both good and bad-bad if the behavior is inconsiderate and dangerous to one's health or well being and good if it is positive and life affirming.

PATRICK: I once looked up the origin of the word 'considerate' and found it was from the Latin meaning to look at closely, observe. It is about being aware of the world around us.

YOSHI: You gave a good example of that when you mentioned that you look behind you as you go out a door. I have a set of qualities of a considerate person that is spelled out in the word 'considerate'. I challenge you to give me an example of an action that would apply.

PATRICK: Okay, Yoshi, go for it.

Yoshi: **The 'C' stands for 'caring.'** The person who is considerate truly cares about other people. How would a person show that?

PATRICK: I am a great believer is remembering the life events of people. I like to send out birthday, anniversary, and even sympathy cards. Some are humorous and others are serious. The people in my life whom I want to express my love for, I send a thoughtful card.

YOSHI: You may even want to think about composing your own greetings but just taking the time to send a card shows people that you care.

YOSHI: **The 'O' stands for 'open.'** If you really are to be considerate, you have to be open to people. By that I mean you can read their moods and emotions. I once worked for a man who we watched every morning to see what mood he was in. If he came in looking grumpy, we stayed away from him for a few hours until he had his three cups of coffee. If he came in smiling, we knew we could approach him. How do you show openness to people, Patrick?

PATRICK: For me it is being a good listener. As priests in training, we knew that we would be hearing confessions as part of our duties. That would require that we listen carefully not only to the words but to the emotions behind those words. I can remember going to confession and my voice was shaky and I was scared about what the father confessor would say to me. My mind would play up my sin so that I knew I was going to hell but the priest often calmed my fears and was understanding. That is a good lesson-be open and understanding.

YOSHI: Many people listen but don't really hear. You must have to want to be a good listener, give verbal and visual clues, and control distractions especially thinking about what you are going to say next instead of listening.

PATRICK: What do you mean by the clues of listening.

YOSHI: You ask questions to clarify points. That let's the person know you are listening. You can also paraphrase what someone is saying to clarify understanding. Visually you can make eye contact, lean in toward the person to show interest and watch your body language, no negative gestures such as crossing your arms.

PATRICK: Wow, I didn't know there was so much involved in listening.

YOSHI: Back to our considerate actions. **The 'N' stands for 'nurturing.** We just have to look at the penguins to learn about nurturing.

PATRICK: I don't know much about penguins, Yoshi.

YOSHI: After laying the egg, the mother very carefully transfers the egg to the male, before immediately returning to the sea for two months to feed. The transfer of the egg can be awkward and difficult, and many couples drop the egg in the process. When this happens, the chick inside is quickly lost, as the egg cannot withstand the freezing temperatures on the icy ground. The male spends the winter incubating the egg in his brood pouch, balancing it on the tops of his feet, for 64 consecutive days until hatching. The Emperor Penguin is the only species where this behaviour is observed; in all other penguin species both parents take shifts incubating.

By the time the egg hatches, the male will have fasted for around 115 days since arriving at the colony. To survive the cold and winds of up to 200 km/h (120 mph), the males huddle together, taking turns in the middle of the huddle. They have also been observed with their backs to the wind to conserve body heat. In the four months of travel, courtship, and incubation, the male may lose as much as 20 kg (44 lb), from around 38 kg to just 18 kg (84 lb to 40 lb).

Hatching may take as long as two or three days to complete, as the shell of the egg is thick. Newly hatched chicks are covered with only a thin layer of down and entirely dependent on their parents for food and warmth.

Emperor Penguin feeding a chick.

The female penguin returns at any time from hatching to ten days afterwards, from mid-July to early August. She finds her mate among the hundreds of fathers by his vocal call and takes over caring for the chick, feeding it by regurgitating the food that she has stored in her stomach. The male then leaves to take his turn at sea, spending around 24 days there before returning. His trip is slightly shorter than it was originally, because the melting of ice in the summer gradually decreases the distance between the breeding site and the open sea. The parents then take turns while the other forages at sea."

PATRICK: Those penguins give new meaning to the word 'nurture.'

YOSHI: When you think about consideration for others, it is about nurturing relationships with people but you have to be **sincere** which is what the **'S' stands for.** It is not about paying lip service but an actual conscious effort."

PATRICK: There is that old saying about talking the talk and walking the walk. For me if I am going to be considerate of others, I have to demonstrate it in my actions such as sending out those greeting cards I mentioned.

YOSHI: There is another element here-not to expect something in return. Today I think too many people want a tit-for-tat. They give but

34

want something back which in reality negates the good they do. It is like volunteering-one can give of one's time freely or be a paid volunteer. Many charitable organizations don't have the money to pay volunteers so their very existence depends of a group of volunteers who work on their own time.

PATRICK: Well, they are paid but not with money. For me it would be the satisfaction of helping in whatever way I can to make someone's life better.

YOSHI: That is something I am sure you learned in the seminary, right?

PATRICK: Yes, but I also remember hearing a speech by President Kennedy who started the Peace Corps. His famous call was to do something yourself without expecting your country to do it for you. He included everyone.

YOSHI: That leads me to the letter **'I' in the word 'considerate'** which stands for **'inclusive.'** The considerate person does not allow prejudice to be the basis of decisions and who to include in his/her life.

PATRICK: I think more and more people are coming to understand the value of inclusiveness. I look at Los Angles which has its diverse population. I enjoy various ethnic foods so I can get Jamaican jerk chicken one day, Thai barbeque the next, or go to a Vietnamese Pho restaurant, enjoy a sushi bar like the Flying Fish, or Roscoe's Waffles and Chicken. The possibilities make my mouth water.

YOSHI: Stop, Patrick, you are making me hungry. The city not only has the foods but the culture of various countries. I enjoy going to Little Tokyo to shop not only for food but stores that have Japanese books and artifacts. I can also go to Koreatown and Little Saigon.

PATRICK: But I wonder, Yoshi, how many people take advantage of this diversity?

YOSHI: That is a very good question, Patrick. It is there for the enjoyment, but there has to be the desire to get out of your comfort zone and explore. That is very much about the American spirit and what led to the founding of the West.

PATRICK: This inclusiveness is evident too in the celebration of the lives of the diverse people who made this country great-not only presidents but people like Martin Luther King and Cesar Chavez. The look of the Congress is changing also with the election of people from different cultures.

YOSHI: Yes, we are including them in the political process which will, I think, be very beneficial to this country. They have had to overcome many obstacles to succeed.

That brings us to **the 'D' in 'considerate' that stands for 'determined.'** You mentioned obstacles which have defeated many a person but having that determination to win at all costs has given us champions. We can call this determination by another word, 'perseverance.' Alexander Graham Bell once said,

> 'What this power is I cannot say; all I know is that it exists and it becomes available only when a man is in that state of mind in which he knows exactly what he wants and is fully determined not to quit until he finds it.'

PATRICK: I would say he was a good model for persistence. Look how the telephone has evolved, and it all began with a man who would not give up.

YOSHI: Thomas Edison is another man who refused to quit ever after he had failed 1,000 times to perfect the electric light bulb. They asked him about why he continued in his quest, and he said that every failure brought him closer to finding a solution because he had found 1,000 ways it didn't work.

PATRICK: A thousand failures? Wow, I wonder how many give up just after one or two. I need to read more biographies of those in history who continued despite the obstacles. They sure can be inspiring.

YOSHI: We do need to learn from those who have gone before us. We also need to ignore the naysayers who tell us that something can't be done. Mark Twain said it well,

'Keep away from people who try to belittle your ambitions. Small people always do that, but the really great make you feel that you, too, can become great.'

PATRICK: You know, Yoshi, I have been fortunate in my life to have people who have encouraged me to pursue my goals and go for what I want in life. We all need people to support us. They are the motivators that help us to persist and stay the course. Many times they have experienced many of the same obstacles so they can identify what we are going through.

YOSHI: You just expressed **the 'E' in 'considerate.'** It is about being **'empathetic.'** It is about walking in someone else's shoes to experience what they have gone through. Have you seen the film "Dances with Wolves"?

PATRICK: I have heard of it but never have seen it.

YOSHI: I suggest you watch it because it is a good example of what being empathetic is all about. Just a quick recap of the plot. It tells the story of a Civil War-era United States Army Lieutenant Dunbar (Kevin Costner) who travels to the American frontier to found a military post, and his dealings with a group of Lakota Indians. Dunbar finds himself drawn to the lifestyle and customs of the tribe, and constantly looks forward to their company. He becomes a hero among the Sioux and is accepted as an honored guest after he locates a migrating herd of buffalo. During the ensuing buffalo hunt, he saves one of the young Indians from a rampaging bull, and at last everyone accepts him as a friend.

Ultimately he saves the tribe by warning them of an imminent attack by the Army so he is considered a traitor and deserter so he goes with the tribe to find another camp.

PATRICK: It sounds like a movie that I would enjoy. It has a message that resonates even today about how we treat people not understanding what they are going through.

YOSHI: This is especially true as the United States becomes more diverse. Before we throw any stones, we need to try to understand where people are coming from which may be from a cultural point of view.

37

PATRICK: That is where the 'consider" comes in. We need to stop and think before we judge others who may be different from ourselves.

YOSHI: Lt. Dunbar got to know the Indians and it changed his entire perspective. He became acquainted with their culture and customs but more importantly their humanity. He learned to respect them and they him which is what the **'R" is in 'considerate", respectful.**

PATRICK: That is something I had to learn, and the seminary helped me do that. One of our subjects in school was the study of comparative religions. I got to learn about other religions, and it was stressed that we needed to respect other beliefs. Many of us found that hard to do because we often are told that a belief is unchangeable.

YOSHI: You know, Patrick, that when I came to the United States, I encountered so many people of different faiths. In Japan, I associated with people who held similar beliefs to mine. By associating with others of different faiths and cultures, it broadened my outlook both towards people and towards life but I had to take the initiative which brings us to the **'A'** in "considerate, **'assertive'** because the considerate person stands up for what he/she believes.

PATRICK: That is not always easy to do, Yoshi. You can look to people throughout history who have suffered for what they believe in. Jesus would be the prime example. He said that a prophet is without honor in his own country, and he predicted that he would be ridiculed and betrayed.

YOSHI: Very true, Patrick. The people we most admire are those who despite great odds triumphed. Martin Luther King, Jr. and Ghandi come to mind right away. Andrew Bernstein said, 'A hero has faced it all: he need not be undefeated, but he must be undaunted.'

PATRICK: That takes courage, Yoshi. I remember as a child I was often made fun of because of my buck teeth and my nick name was 'Bucky Beaver' after the beaver in the toothpaste commercials. At first I wanted to run and hide and avoid the taunts, but then I realized that they would not stop unless I did something about them. So I began to make fun of myself by singing the theme to that toothpaste commercial and sticking my teeth out. The kids loved it, laughed and the taunts stopped.

YOSHI: Sounds like you learned a lesson early in life to take control of a situation instead of it taking control of you. You asserted yourself. Someone once said that he would rather die on his feet than on his knees-standing for something.

PATRICK: Yes, like they say, if you don't stand for something, you will fall for anything.

YOSHI: Patrick, you have a lot of wisdom for such a young man. I am sure it is because you think a lot about life. A considerate person is also **thoughtful**-the **T** in considerate.

PATRICK: I do owe that quality to my seminary education because we were taught to put others first and think of our own needs last.

YOSHI: What are some ways that we can show that thoughtfulness?

PATRICK: The freeways give me lots of opportunity to do that?

YOSHI: How so?

PATRICK: These ramps where people have to merge into traffic. I usually allow space to let someone in the lane. I also keep a space between myself and the next car which is not only thoughtful but a safe practice because I read where following too closely is the cause of most accidents.

YOSHI: I wish there were more thoughtful people driving these days. There are too many examples of people not thinking too-talking on their cells phones while driving, being distracted by paying attention to something in the vehicle and not on the driving.

PATRICK: I've seen people eating, looking at maps and even newspapers while driving. You know they are concentrating on something else and not their driving. No wonder insurance rates are so high. You also mentioned something new referred to as RAD.

YOSHI: Random Acts of Kindness. People for no reason at all except to be thoughtful doing something nice for someone.

PATRICK: Can you give me some examples, Yoshi?

YOSHI: You can send a greeting card to someone telling them that you are thinking about them or wishing them a good day or a thank you card to express appreciation besides doing it at Thanksgiving. Writing a letter or calling someone whom you haven't talked to in a long time. These small acts may have great impacts on people's lives. We don't know what trials people are going through and a small act of kindness may even save a life.

PATRICK: They may not be so small. I like the idea of the randomness of them. You do it without a reason or occasion. I can see where that would touch someone more when it is least expected.

YOSHI: There is also another aspect of this, Patrick. You are staying involved in the lives of people which brings us to the final letter of 'considerate' '**E**' stands for '**engage**'-actively seek out people most in need, get off the couch. President Theodore Roosevelt was a fan of boxing and one of his most famous quotes about being engaged uses a boxing analogy.

'It is not the critic who counts, not the man who points out how the strong man stumbled, or where the doer of deed could have done them better. The credit belongs to the man who is actually in the arena; whose face is marred by dust and sweat and blood; who strives valiantly; who errs and comes short again and again; who knows the great enthusiasm, the devotions, and spends himself in a worthy cause; who at best, knows in the end the triumph of high achievement; and who, at the worst, if he fails, at least fails while daring greatly, so that his place shall never be with those cold and timid souls who know neither victory nor defeat.'

PATRICK: That is a very graphic description, Yoshi but it reminds me that if we are out there in the world, we may get hurt but the alternative is not getting involved and not experiencing what life has to offer. That is part of the reason I left the seminary.

YOSHI: Tell me about that, Patrick.

PATRICK: I was fourteen years old when I went in and knew little of life. The seminary life is a very sheltered one so I was shielded from all the events in life. We were allowed to watch one half hour of television a night and it was the nightly news. That was really the only contact we had with the outside world except for letters from the family. When I came home during the summer vacation, I was suddenly engaged in a world that I had no experience in.

YOSHI: It must have been awkward for you having to deal with secular things rather than religious.

PATRICK: It was. Contact with girls was a really hard time for me. They would be afraid to approach me because they already saw me as a priest and not a person. We forget that priests are human and have feelings and emotions.

YOSHI: As a teen, Patrick, those emotions may even be stronger as you were finding your way in the world.

PATRICK: I wanted to engage but shied away from it. After I left the seminary, it took me a while to feel comfortable around people. At first my consideration of others was more from fear than any deliberate act. I did not pay attention to the problems of others and wonder what the consequences of my disengagement were.

YOSHI: Let me tell you the story about the mouse. This will clarify for you the consequences that you are talking about.

A mouse looked through the crack in the wall
to see the farmer and his wife open a package.
"What food might this contain?" The mouse wondered.
He was devastated to discover it was a mousetrap.

Retreating to the farmyard,
the mouse proclaimed this warning :
 "There is a mousetrap in the house!
There is a mousetrap in the house!"

The chicken clucked and scratched,
raised her head and said, "Mr. Mouse,
I can tell this is a grave concern to you,
but it is of no consequence to me.
I cannot be bothered by it."
The mouse turned to the pig and told him,
"There is a mousetrap in the house!
There is a mousetrap in the house!"

The pig sympathized, but said,
"I am so very sorry, Mr. Mouse,
but there is nothing I can do about it
but pray.
Be assured you are in my prayers."

The mouse turned to the cow and said,
"There is a mousetrap in the house!
There is a mousetrap in the house!"

The cow said, "Wow, Mr. Mouse. I'm sorry for you,
but it's no skin off my nose."

So, the mouse returned to the house,
head down and dejected,
to face the farmer's mousetrap
. . .. Alone. . .

That very night
a sound was heard throughout the house
-- the sound of a mousetrap catching its prey.

The farmer's wife rushed to see what was caught.
In the darkness, she did not see it.
It was a venomous snake
whose tail was caught in the trap.

The snake bit the farmer's wife.
The farmer rushed her to the hospital.

When she returned home she still had a fever.
Everyone knows you treat a fever
with fresh chicken soup.
So the farmer took his hatchet to the farmyard
for the soup's main ingredient:
But his wife's sickness continued.
Friends and neighbors
came to sit with her
around the clock.
To feed them,
the farmer butchered the pig.

But, alas,
the farmer's wife did not get well...
She died.

So many people came for her funeral
that the farmer had the cow slaughtered
to provide enough meat for all of them
for the funeral luncheon.

And the mouse looked upon it all
from his crack in the wall
with great sadness.

So, the next time you hear
someone is facing a problem
and you think it doesn't concern you,
remember ---

When one of us is threatened, we are all at risk.
We are all involved in this journey called life.
We must keep an eye out for one another

and make an extra effort
to encourage one another.

PATRICK: That is some story and with a good moral. So the consideration we have talked about is about keeping an eye out for each other and to be encouraging. I think it has to do with that interconnectedness-we all are connected in some way to each other.

YOSHI: Yes, Patrick, it is like thinking of others as family because we are the family of human beings all sharing planet Earth. The problems of others are also our problems. It goes back to the Golden Rule and doing unto others what you would like done to you.

PATRICK: I will remember the mouse story and pass it on. It is a keeper. I am off to the gym. Later, Yoshi.

Yoshi's Yardsticks for Success:
Set a goal to perform three considerate acts for others in the coming week. Write them below.

Considerate Act 1:

Considerate Act 2:

Considerate Act 3:

Thought of the Day:

"What do we live for, if it is not to make life less difficult for each other?"

George Eliot (1819-1880)

Seed 6. Silence is Good for the Soul

THE SCENE

Patrick receives an invitation to visit Yoshi's house in Long Beach. Using his GPS system, he finds the street and address but the house is a guest house behind the main structure. Patrick notices the beautiful landscaping as he walks along the path to the back house. He knows that gardening is not just a job for Yoshi but a labor of love.

Patrick rings the bell but receives no response so he walks behind the guest house where Yoshi is kneeling in the middle of what appears to be a prayer garden with an altar with incense and candles and a statue of Buddha. He stands quietly while Yoshi continues his meditation.

Yoshi sensing Patrick's presence, stands and bows to the Buddha and turns slowly to greet Patrick.

YOSHI: Good day, Patrick. I thought it would be good to talk here today to avoid interruptions. Would you like some tea?

PATRICK: I would like that very much. It is so quiet back here that I forget that you are in a residential neighborhood.

YOSHI: Yes, even in a city we can find peace and quiet. It is similar to your seminary experience I would gather.

PATRICK: Yes, we did have a lot of peace and quiet especially during that night silence period from 7:30 in the evening until at the end of breakfast the next morning.

YOSHI: I remember you saying that you didn't care much for that time.

PATRICK: For me it was not so much about the time but the lack of communication. There were times I wanted to scream just to break the monotony. Other times I thought of things I wanted to share with my classmates but couldn't say anything.

YOSHI: For a teen, that must have been hard. You have all that energy but must contain it. What do you think, Patrick, was the purpose of that night silence?

PATRICK: Looking back on it now, I see the value as related to discipline. It taught us to control ourselves and created an atmosphere in which we could study and pray and get a good night's sleep too. But by the time it ended after breakfast, we burst out of the refectory like an explosion.

YOSHI: The silence allowed you to turn inward and reflect more personally on yourself rather than others and prevented distractions. You mentioned study.

PATRICK: Yes, we had a study hall before rosary in the evening and the silence was very good for concentration though some boys tried a few tricks to break up the atmosphere but the deacons were there as monitors so it was an effective time.

YOSHI: I am amazed that there seems to be less silent time today and the noise of the world intrudes on our everyday activities. There are televisions everywhere even in restaurants where many people just want to enjoy a quiet meal. I see people constantly talking on cell phones and kids with music devices in their ears even when they are studying. I wonder if they ever get any quiet time at all?

PATRICK: I have stopped by a church during the day and saw many older people just sitting or kneeling. I think they go to get way from all the noise and spend some quiet time together.

YOSHI: Yes, there seems to be fewer places to get away. That is why I have created this space for myself.

PATRICK: You have a beautiful place to sit and enjoy the silence.

YOSHI: There is another element to silence that is important to communication and that is listening. There are time when we need to just be quiet and listen to both our inner self and others. I think that if we listened more, we would help each other more.

PATRICK: I once heard someone say that the reason God gave us two ears and one mouth is that we should listen twice as much as talk.

YOSHI: One of our presidents, LBJ, said that he never learned anything by talking. Listening is actually a skill and there are rules for active listening.

PATRICK: I never heard of any rules, Yoshi, will you share them with me?

YOSHI: I have broken them down into helpful vs. disruptive behaviors. For example, asking questions is helpful and the best to ask are open-ended questions. Good questions involve people; bring out experience, opinions, and expertise; there is an art to asking questions effectively. They are open ended; ask questions like what, when, how, why; stimulate thinking and ask for an opinion; continue to probe for answers.

Bad questions can only be answered by yes or no; they are leading questions.

Disruptive behavior would be interrupting when someone is talking. Many times we are thinking about what we are going to say rather than truly listening."

PATRICK: People seem to be in a rush to get their opinions out and ignore those of others.

YOSHI: You are right. Another helpful behavior is withholding judgment. It is important to listen until the person makes his/her case before judging. Too many times we make snap judgments which are disruptive.

PATRICK: That is especially true about how we seem to make judgments about people.

YOSHI: You are talking about stereotyping, I think.

PATRICK: Yes, we need to listen more rather than make up our minds based on a person's look. It reminds me of the story of the young man who picked up a hitchhiker who was dressed very poorly and had not shaved. He talked crazy and the driver made the assumption that he was some poor, homeless person. It turned out that the man was Howard Hughes.

YOSHI: (laughing). That paid off for the young man, right?

PATRICK: Yes, Hughes left him money in his will, I believe.

YOSHI: Another good listening behavior is concentrating on the speaker. There are ways to do this. I notice you tend to look me in the eyes which is a good indicator that you are listening. Another is body language-open stance with arms not folded and leaning in toward the speaker. The disruptive behaviors would be looking away from the speaker, checking out the time, or anything that takes away from being fully engaged with the speaker.

PATRICK: I never realized that there was so much to listening.

YOSHI: That's why we call it 'active listening' because you make a concerted effort, Patrick, to really hear what the other person is communicating. Another good behavior is finding common ground. If you can relate to what the speaker is saying, you will be a better listener. It will keep you from being bored because the speaker has something that interests you.

PATRICK: I think that would take some work but the payoff would be that you connect.

YOSHI: That connection is important in order to have effective communication. There is a need there also to separate intent and content.

PATRICK: What is that about, Yoshi?

YOSHI: I did some acting in Japan and one of the skills an actor must learn is understanding the subtext of the dialogue. What is going on between the lines? Many times we only pay attention to the facts and not the intent of the communication. For example, at a meeting the CEO may be giving out lots of financial information but the true intent of the meeting is to prove that the company may not be doing that well and that cost cutting is coming.

PATRICK: That too takes work because you really have to concentrate to be able to find underlying meaning. The two ears will certainly come in handy.

YOSHI: There are ways, Patrick, to show understanding. One way is by paraphrasing: repeating back in your own words what the other person said and showing understanding of why the person feels the way he or she does. If your purpose is to understand content, then make statements such as:
'It sounds like you're saying....'
'As I understand it so far, you're saying....'
'My understanding of what you're saying is....'
'So far, what you are focusing on is....'

If your purpose is to acknowledge feelings, then say:
'You're (feeling)_____because (reason)_____.'

'It sounds like you're (feeling)_____because (reason)_____.'

'You seem (feeling)_____about (situation)_____.'

As you can see, Patrick there is quite a lot involved in active listening.

PATRICK: It makes me wonder, Yoshi, how much I have missed in people's communication because I didn't check for understanding.

YOSHI: I would think that most people don't listen that well. There is another aspect of silence that is important to understand and that is in regard to not speaking up when you should.

PATRICK: I'm not sure I understand that.

YOSHI: Let me give you an example. There are times when you find yourself in a situation where you have to decide to speak up or not. Let's say you are working in a warehouse and you see a fellow employee stealing merchandise. Do you say something or let it go because you do not want to cause trouble?

PATRICK: I think you are referring to an ethical dilemma. The person knows stealing is wrong but doesn't want to see the person lose his/her job. I would take the person aside and tell him of the consequences and see if he stops.

YOSHI: And if he doesn't heed your advice?

PATRICK: Then I would have to report it because if I didn't, I would be an accomplice.

YOSHI: You are right, Patrick. Your silence could lead to dire consequences for you too. So there are times when silence is good and other times inappropriate. There is a phrase in the Bible, 'by their silence they shout.' There are times when keeping silent makes a statement. Can you think of an example?

PATRICK: It makes me think of the term 'biting your tongue' when you want to say something but hold back. In the case of making a statement by not speaking, I think of times when you do not cast a vote as a statement of protest.

YOSHI: Did you ever hear the term The Silent Majority, Patrick?

PATRICK: No.

(Yoshi brings in a laptop and goes to Wikipedia, Patrick reads the following)

> "The **silent majority** is an unspecified large majority of people in a country or group who do not express their opinions publicly. The term was popularized (though not first used) by President Richard Nixon in a November 3, 1969 speech, where it referred to those Americans who did not join in the large demonstrations against the Vietnam War at the time, who did not join in the counterculture, and who did not enthusiastically participate in public discourse or the media. Nixon along with many others saw this group as being overshadowed by the more vocal minority.

This majority referred mainly to the older generation (those World War II Veterans in all parts of the United States) but it also described many young people in the Midwest, West and in the South, many of whom did eventually serve in Vietnam. The Silent Majority was mostly populated with the blue collar people who allegedly didn't have the ability or the time to take an active part in politics other than to vote. They did, in some cases, support the conservative policies of many politicians. Others were not particularly conservative politically, but resented what they saw as disrespect for American institutions.

The silent majority theme has been a contentious issue amongst journalists since Nixon used the phrase. Some thought Nixon used it as part of the Southern strategy; others claim it was Nixon's way of dismissing the obvious protests going on around the country, and Nixon's attempt to get other Americans not to listen to the protests. Whatever the rationale, Nixon won a landslide victory in 1972, taking 49 of 50 states, vindicating his silent majority."

PATRICK: I think that today that majority is now a minority as we seem to have lost the silence. Everyone wants to put his/her two cents in. I see so many talk shows today which makes me wonder if anyone is silent today.

YOSHI: Monks may be the last silent group left, Patrick.

PATRICK: I've done my silent time but now I do it consciously in meditation. I think there is still room for silence in the world.

YOSHI: Maybe more than ever we need to listen to the sounds of silence as Simon and Garfunkle sang years ago.

PATRICK: Yoshi, you have a good grasp of musical history.

YOSHI: I admire music as the expression of our feelings and emotions. For myself, music can enhance the silence.

PATRICK: I will leave you to your quiet time here. You have been a gracious host. Thank you and I'll see you soon at the gardens.

YOSHI: It was a pleasure, Patrick as always. Let me show you to the door.

Yoshi's Yardsticks for Success:
Set a goal to become a more active listener this week. Write what you will do below.

Active Listening Goal 1:

_____

Active Listening Goal 2:

_____

Active Listening Goal 3:

_____

Thought of the Day:

"Deep listening is miraculous for both listener and speaker. When someone receives us with open-hearted, non-judging, intensely interested listening, our spirits expand."

Sue Patton Thoele

Seed 7. Learning to Live with Simplicity

Patrick meets Yoshi a few days later at the gardens. Yoshi is on lunch break so Patrick sits on the bench waiting for him to finish his lunch.

YOSHI: Would you care so share some of my sandwich, Patrick?

PATRICK: Thanks, Yoshi. I just had lunch. Something I noticed about your house is that it was really sparsely furnished but elegant in its simplicity.

YOSHI: The first time we met, I was trimming a banzai tree. Do you remember?

PATRICK: Yes, I do and I remember remarking that we all probably needed to do a little trimming.

YOSHI: Yes, Patrick. That was an astute observation because only by cutting back does the tree thrive. Does that relate to anything from you seminary days?

PATRICK: Now that I think about it, we lived very simple lives. We didn't own much, just the clothes and a few toiletries. We didn't have any electronic gadgets or entertainment paraphernalia such as DVDs or CDs.

YOSHI: Did you miss any of that?

PATRICK: No. We knew that part of the training for becoming priests was to reject worldly things. I never felt in anyway that I was being deprived.

YOSHI: Why do you think that was?

PATRICK: Our focus was elsewhere.

YOSHI: What was it that you were focusing on?

PATRICK: We concentrated on our spiritual and academic lives. I think those other things would have been a distraction. We were so involved that we had no time to miss anything else.

YOSHI: Albert Einstein said:

>'Out of clutter, find simplicity.
>From discord, find harmony.
>In the middle of difficulty, lies opportunity.'

It's this clutter that keeps us, in my opinion, from realizing our true potential. Do you know what the fastest growing business is?

PATRICK: Considering what we are talking about, I would think it has something to do with clutter.

YOSHI: Yes, it does. It is the increase of public storage units where we can store all that clutter. Along with this, there is another business and that is helping people simplify their lives.

PATRICK: How interesting, Yoshi, that on the one hand we buy everything in sight and on the other, get rid of it or shove it into storage.

YOSHI: I think we as a race are beginning to understand that happiness does not come from material things because they do not last. So what are the things that will remain even if we lose everything?

PATRICK: Well, for me it would be the relationships of family and friends and my own abilities which are inside me not the outside trappings.

YOSHI: Lucille Clifton said:

> 'What will see me through the next 20 years
> (and I am less sure of those 20 than I was of
> 'forever')
> Is my knowledge that even in the face of
> The sweeping away of all that I assumed
> To be permanent, even when the universe
> Makes it quite clear to me that I was mistaken
> In my certainties, in my definitions, I did not break.
> The shattering of my sureties did not shatter me.
> Stability comes from inside, not outside....'"

PATRICK: Yoshi, she made a good point when she said that she assumed those things would be permanent. It reminds me of what people say when they have lost everything due to a natural disaster such as a tornado or earthquake. They remark that things can be replaced but a life cannot so that the lives of those around them are more important.

YOSHI: It sometimes takes a disaster to put things in perspective. We seem secure but in reality we are not. Anne Morrow Lindbergh said:

'Only in growth, reform and change, paradoxically enough,
 Is true security to be found.'

PATRICK: I would argue about change though. Most people would say that change is not about security. If you look at the number of people losing jobs and facing a tough economy, for them change does not mean security.

YOSHI: So do you see change as bad, Patrick?

PATRICK: Not necessarily but often times it causes hardship for people going through it.

YOSHI: There are ways of managing change.

PATRICK: How can I manage change, Yoshi?

YOSHI: Think of the letters in the word 'change' and use them as your guide. (C=confidence, H=honesty, A=adapt, N=new opportunities, G=growth, E=esteem)

You must have **Confidence** in your self that you can handle change. Think about your past experience with change and how you were able to handle it; for example, coming out of the seminary into the secular world.

PATRICK: Now that was some change. I came out of a very controlled environment into one that I had so much freedom of choice that I didn't know how to handle it, but my training allowed me to put things in perspective. I was able to handle it.

YOSHI: So use that same confidence in facing the many changes you will encounter in your life. The 'H' is for **honesty**. You must be honest with yourself and not be deceived into thinking that change is easy. It isn't.

PATRICK: I know that. I think it is about facing the reality of change that it does turns life upside down sometimes. We can kid ourselves that change is not the normal way of life but in today's world, change is happening constantly.

YOSHI: Why do you think that?

PATRICK: I think there are forces in the world causing this to happen such as changing technology and the population in general.

YOSHI: How so?

PATRICK: When I came to LA, I was so surprised at the diversity I found here. To be honest, in the seminary there was not much diversity. All my classmates were white boys from pretty well off families. I am sure there will be major changes the ordained priests will go through when they get to their parishes and find such diversity.

YOSHI: Yes, the world is changing quickly and unless we change with it, we will be left in the dust so to speak. That brings us to the '**a**' which is **adapt**. Change causes us to take a look at ourselves and the qualities we have that can help us adapt. Do you think you have some of those qualities, Patrick?

PATRICK: If I am correct, it is a quality like self-confidence that will help me adapt to the changes. I know that I am a pretty even-tempered person who doesn't allow little things to upset me.

YOSHI: That is a good quality because changes shake us out of our comfort zones sometimes so you have to have a thick skin and not let them throw you off your game.

PATRICK: I think too about work today which is so different from when my father was in the workforce. He stayed in the same career all his life-textile manufacturing but right after he retired, the industry went off shore and most of the mills he worked with in New England are now condos or museums.

YOSHI: That is a change that is affecting millions of people but with change comes **new opportunities**-the '**n**'. I like the line from 'The Sound of Music" when Maria says that when God closes a window, he opens a door.

PATRICK: That is one of my favorite films because I can identify with her leaving the religious environment and being literally thrown into the real world. She had a lot of adapting to do with the kids, falling in love, and the politics of emerging Nazi power. That was a lot to cope with.

YOSHI: Yes, but she was able to handle it due to her faith and confidence. She even sings about having that confidence in herself. Another aspect of change is that it helps us to **grow** which is the '**g**.' One of my favorite sayings is that when you are green you grow, when you are ripe, you rot.

PATRICK: As a gardener I can see where that would be a favorite of yours, but it also has a lot of truth. For me the message is to keep growing and changes help us to grow as a person if we see them as opportunities.

YOSHI: Unfortunately, Patrick, many people see change as negative not as a positive so your perception of change is very important.

PATRICK: Since we have been talking about simplicity, that is something that change does for us-simplify our lives which is especially true if our income is affected by change.

YOSHI: That too can be perceived as good or bad, Patrick. Losing a job at first is devastating to most people but those who adapt may find an opportunity to do something that they have always wanted to do in life.

PATRICK: I thought leaving the seminary was going to lead to depression but once I had some time away, I realized that it was just the closing of one chapter of my life and that I would be writing the next chapter.

YOSHI: These changes will help us achieve new goals and that will in turn raise our **esteem** which is the 'e.' Here in the gardens I have met people who have lost jobs and feel that their lives have ended because their identity was tied to their jobs. After talking with them, they realize that they have the power in themselves to overcome adversity and once they do that, their self-esteem soars.

PATRICK: I have a saying I carry with me. Let me read it to you. The author is John Dewy.

> *'Since changes are going on anyway, the great thing is to learn enough about them so that we will be able to lay hold of them and turn them in the direction of our desires. Conditions and events are neither to be fled from nor passively acquiesced in; they are to be utilized and directed.'*

YOSHI: Patrick, that is very inspiring. I especially like the part about turning them in the direction of our desires. In that phrase is the essence of what we are talking about, taking control and making them work for us.

PATRICK: Yoshi, as usual this has been a very enlightening exchange and I thank you for that. Let's talk again soon. I am going to think more about simplifying my life and taking control of the changes that are going on in my life right now.

YOSHI: Great, Patrick. I think I will go put on Bob Dylan's song, 'Times they are a changing.' That will inspire me.

PATRICK: I am more into David Bowie's 'Changes' but we both have some music to get us thinking. See you soon.

Yoshi's Yardsticks for Success:
What can you do to simplify your life? What change are you going through and how will you adapt?

Trimming 1:

_____

Trimming 2:

_____

What changes are you experiencing and how will you handle them?

_____
_____
_____
_____
_____
_____
_____

Thought of the day:

"In character, in manners, in style, in all things, the supreme excellence is simplicity."
Longfellow

Seed 8. Basic Black is a Fashion Statement

THE SCENE

Patrick is sitting in Yoshi's house sipping tea on a Saturday afternoon. They sit in silence listening to the water cascading in the fountain and the birds chirping. Patrick feels very comfortable in this environment.

YOSHI: Something I have noticed about you, Patrick, is that you are not very much into fashion like most of today's young people. You do not have any piercings and your clothes are not flashy.

PATRICK: I am not a trendy person, Yoshi. After six years of wearing only black, I do not have much of a fashion sense. I prefer to be comfortable, not fashionable.

YOSHI: Does the name Marlee Matlin mean anything to you?

PATRICK: No, I don't recall ever hearing about her.

YOSHI: She starred in a very touching film, *Children of a Lesser God* about a teacher who helps hearing impaired children speak and sing. I highly recommend you watch this film especially since you are considering a career in teaching.

PATRICK: I will check out the DVD.

YOSHI: I mention her, Patrick, because she once said this:

'It seems we're always in transition and that it's more about trends that it is about what's meaningful.'

It bothers me that people today seem to care more about the trendy than what is meaningful.

PATRICK: Maybe I am lucky, Yoshi, that I have never been into fads.

YOSHI: Yes, your seminary training led you to care not about what you wore but what you stood for. The Bible admonishes us not to care less about what we put on but what we are doing.

PATRICK: Why do you think people are so caught up in being fashionable?

YOSHI: I once heard a phrase, Patrick, about keeping up with the Joneses. I never knew what it meant until I moved into the neighborhood and heard the neighbors talking about what someone next door had purchased and the need for them to buy the same.

PATRICK: The flaw in that thinking, Yoshi, is that people are tying their success and self-esteem on what they have materially.

YOSHI: Living here in the land of fires, floods, and earthquakes should dispel any thought about security being in what we own because it can be wiped out in a matter of seconds.

PATRICK: It's interesting that when people are interviewed after a disaster, they usually say that they are fortunate to be alive. The focus shifts from what they own to their lives.

YOSHI: It is unfortunate, Patrick, that it takes a catastrophe to make us realize what is important in life. Another thought occurs to me that we are bombarded with images and ads everywhere we go.

PATRICK: I hear that. Taking a drive down Sunset Blvd. and there are billboards galore. The messages are interesting though. It seems that if you use a certain perfume, you will find love or you can get the girl if you use a certain cologne.

YOSHI: Do you really think people buy that product thinking they will find happiness?

66

PATRICK: No, but I do believe they want to identify with the person who is selling the product. Celebrity endorsements are big business.

YOSHI: So I take it you would not buy a product because George Clooney endorses it?

PATRICK: You are right but if the product is beneficial in some way like for my health, I would at least try it.

YOSHI: You live close to Hollywood which has a reputation for being all glamour and no substance. Do you think that is deserved, Patrick?

PATRICK: Partly but overall, I think that being fashionable is more about acceptance by society than trendy. I remember walking down Hollywood Blvd. for the first time and being shocked by the array of styles I encountered-people dressed in all manner of clothing more costume than custom and hair colors and styles that were outrageous. Having come from the almost sterile atmosphere of the seminary, it was a real culture shock for me.

YOSHI: I can only imagine. There is another aspect of this fashion and that is being daring to be different. It goes back to Thoreau who said to march to the beat of the drum you hear.

PATRICK: Well, Yoshi, some people surely do hear a different drum but it may also be about self-expression, about being themselves.

YOSHI: That, I think, goes back to the social movement of the 60's when Haight-Ashbury was the center of a cultural revolution in California and moved to other parts of the United States.

PATRICK: Come to think of it, I have seen some tie-dyed t-shirts lately. Someone once said not to throw anything away as it will always come back into fashion.

YOSHI: Going back to the 60's, the Beatles had a great influence on our culture. I remember boys sporting Paul Mc Cartney haircuts and wearing the suits the group wore.

PATRICK: It is interesting, Yoshi, how different generations rediscover the past. The current youth have rediscovered the Beatles who are selling as many records today as they did in the 60's. There must be something there.

YOSHI: Music resonates across generations. I don't think love songs or beautiful ballads go out of favor. It is not so much about being trendy in this case.

PATRICK: I agree. I listen to the music of past decades because it has the ability to comfort me and at times inspire me. I would never criticize someone's taste in music. My dad had a favorite saying about having different taste which was, 'To each his own said the old maid kissing the cow.'"

YOSHI: I won't be kissing any cows anytime soon, but I think it is important to respect everyone's uniqueness whether it be in music or dress.

PATRICK: (laughing) I won't either but I am comfortable with myself and my choices.

YOSHI: That is a good point about choice. When it comes right down to it, it is about choice and making decisions.

PATRICK: I've had to make some major decisions in my life. At fourteen I decided to leave home and follow Him which at that age is really a major move. Every year I had to decide to return or not and finally the biggest of all, leaving the seminary.

YOSHI: You've made decisions that were life altering and not many young people have to do that. The most important decision most young people need to make is where to go to college. Yours was certainly important to the direction of your life because it was about leaving a career path and heading out on a very different road.

PATRICK: You know, Yoshi, I was not afraid at all about making that decision. I did give it a lot of thought and sought the advice of my spiritual advisor and my parents. In the end though, it was my own. One thing about decisions you have to take the consequences.

YOSHI: Did you consider the consequences?

PATRICK: I did. One was disappointing my parents who like many Irish families hoped to have a son or daughter enter the religious life. The more I thought about that, the more I realized that I would disappoint myself more if I did not follow my heart. I was confident that my family would support me.

YOSHI: Having support when making a momentous decision can be the difference in the outcome. I think about my own decision to come to this country. I too had to leave family and friends but I had a vision of my future.

PATRICK: Another consequence for me was having to decide on a new career path. I was suddenly confronted with so many choices that I was at a loss as to what field to enter.

YOSHI: You came from an environment where everything was being decided for you to one where you had to make a decision. The can be very daunting for a young person, Patrick.

PATRICK: For me just choosing clothes to wear was a major decision. It was about adapting to a new way of life. How do you handle making decisions, Yoshi?

YOSHI: Well, first I identify and define the issue and its boundaries clearly. This also means identifying who else needs to be involved in the issue, and analyzing what their involvement means. You did that when you made the decision to leave the seminary. You sought out the people who were involved-your spiritual counselor and your family. Here are some tips that will help you in making future decisions.

1. You need to approach different types of decisions in different ways for good results. For example, some decisions will be life changing others will be life enhancing. Your decision to leave the seminary was life changing, your decision to go to further your education is life enhancing.

2. If you are having problems making a decision, change your perspective. You need to look at the outcome of the decision. That will help you look at it in a different way.

3. Be aware of who will be affected by your decision. You have a group of people around you who will be affected by the

decisions you make. It does not mean make the decision to please them but take into account how they will react and if it will impact them in any way.

4. Once a decision is clear, make it quickly rather than slowly. In your case, Patrick, the decision to leave the seminary had to be made slowly because it required much thought and prayer. Some people take a long time to make a decision and could lose out on opportunities that could be there if they decided quickly. Going back to the first tip-make a life changing decision slowly but a life enhancing decision quickly.

5. Avoid rushing an important decision just because others expect it. You may be pushed into making a decision because people want you to move on but it is not about them, it is about you and your life so take the time you need to make the best decision for you.

6. Involve as many people as you need in making a decision. Again you did that when you made that decision about the seminary. People often ask how many people should they consult? I tell them whatever they need. That is their decision and only they know how much help they need to make it.

PATRICK: Yoshi, those are great tips. I took notes and will use them. Someone once said that education without application is useless. I really need to put into practice all the good advice you have given me.

YOSHI: Also Patrick there is another element to decision making and that is in the implementation. You are right that unless you take the action, the process won't do you any good. I have a riddle for you: three frogs are sitting on the lily pad. One decides to jump off. How many are left on the lily pad?

PATRICK: Two.

YOSHI: You answered too quickly. That is one time you should think before you leap, so to speak. No, there are three frogs on the lily pad. Why?

(Patrick takes a minute.)

PATRICK: I get it, Yoshi, there are three because a decision is not an action. So the frog decided to jump off but did not actually jump.

YOSHI: Exactly. That is why the implementation is so important and here are a few tips. When you have followed the decision-making process and the moment of decision finally arrives, go back over your options, and consult those you respect. Once you are fully convinced, go ahead.

PATRICK: What about if I find the decision was not the right one?

YOSHI: Monitor your progress, and if the decision is not the right one, identify the reasons and redefine your decision. Always be prepared for unexpected events to affect your plans and be prepared to change your plan of action as new circumstances arise.

PATRICK: I think that sometimes it is difficult to know if the decision was right or not. Sometimes it takes years of hindsight. I am still wondering if I made the right decision about leaving the seminary.

YOSHI: That is natural, Patrick, but does it feel right to you? Only you can know that.

PATRICK: Yes, it does feel right.

YOSHI: Then put your mind at ease. You don't have to wear black anymore unless you want to.

PATRICK: (laughs) Now I remember how this conversation started. It was about how I dressed and my lack of fashion. I guess it will take me a while to catch on but as you said, it is my decision. Time to head out. Thanks for the tea and empathy.

YOSHI: You are welcome anytime. You may want to stop by the GAP.

(both laughing)

PATRICK: Maybe I will, Yoshi, makeovers seem to be big these days.

Yoshi's Yardsticks for Success:

Do something this week that is meaningful, not trendy. What will it be?_____

_____
_____
_____

Watch an inspiring film-what film will you watch this week?

_____
_____
_____
_____

Thought of the day:
    "Success based on anything but internal fulfillment is bound to be empty."
                                    Dr. Martha Friedman

Seed 9. Character is Who You Are!

THE SCENE:

It is a beautiful spring day and perfect for walking around the gardens so Patrick drives to the Huntington. It is not only about enjoying the day, but he wants to talk to Yoshi again. He finds his exchanges with the man clarifies the past and focuses on the future. Being new to the Los Angeles area, he has not made many friends so his time with Yoshi fills a void.

Yoshi is in the rose garden watering the plants which in this climate bloom many times a year. Patrick feels that he too is blooming but needs some nurturing.

PATRICK: Good morning, Yoshi. How are you?

YOSHI: Enjoying the day.

PATRICK: I notice you are wearing a Superman t-shirt. I am surprised to see you wearing a shirt with a comic book character, Yoshi.

YOSHI: Did you ever stop to think that we call them characters and seem to admire them. Why is that?

PATRICK: In the case of Superman, I think it has a lot to do with the qualities that the character has.

YOSHI: What is it that makes him so popular?

PATRICK: He has super human powers which place him above us mortals.

YOSHI: What are some of those powers?

PATRICK: Well, he has that super strength, super vision, and he can fly.

YOSHI: But there is an element to his character that overshadows all those super powers and that is his sense of justice and his focus on helping people.

PATRICK: Yes, he is using his powers in a positive way. I would say he is a role model for us in that respect.

YOSHI: Though he is a comic book character, he has character traits we can emulate. Wouldn't you say?

PATRICK: Of course we don't have super powers.

YOSHI: I wouldn't say that, Patrick. Have you heard the story of the mother who picks up a car to free her child that is trapped underneath? Didn't she use super power?

PATRICK: Yes, but that was an extraordinary situation.

YOSHI: True, but she still was able to harness that power. Don't you think we humans are capable of doing that? It doesn't have to be physical. Many studies have shown that the mind is very powerful. Did you ever see Uri Geller bend a spoon by using the power of his mind?

PATRICK: But wasn't that some kind of parlor trick?

YOSHI: Was it? People who have seen him do it swear that there was no trick involved.

PATRICK: I'd have to see it for myself to believe.

YOSHI: (laughs) Doubting Patrick.

PATRICK: Sure I am skeptical. Seeing is believing.

YOSHI: What ever happened to faith?

PATRICK: There are some things I have faith in but levitating objects and bending spoons are not credible to me.

YOSHI: Fair enough but getting back to our character, there are enough examples to make us believe that we humans have more strength than we give ourselves credit for. Think of all the people who have overcome disasters and survived. Where does that come from?

PATRICK: I think it comes from inside us. It is a combination of belief and confidence. If we have that conviction that we can overcome any adversity, then we can.

YOSHI: Do you think Superman had that belief and confidence initially?

PATRICK: No, I think he had to discover his powers and then by using them, gained the belief and confidence.

YOSHI: So we have to search within ourselves for that inner strength which we then can manifest outwardly.

PATRICK: That is a good way to explain it, but we still have our limitations.

YOSHI: Yes, just as Superman did in the form of Kryptonite. I see that as the negativity that surrounds us limiting our potential to use that power we all have.

PATRICK: How do you overcome that negativity, Yoshi?

YOSHI: It comes from changing our words, our attitudes, and sometimes the people we hang out with.

PATRICK: I sure know how powerful words are. It was the words of encouragement that led me to the seminary. My family, my teachers, and priests all telling me I had what it takes to be a priest which gave me the confidence to pursue that vocation.

YOSHI: Do you think you would ever have taken that path if they had told you that you were not good enough or not worthy to follow in Christ's footsteps?

PATRICK: No, I would have gone to public high school and been on a different career track.

YOSHI: What does attitude have to do with negativity?

PATRICK: I can see where a positive attitude is needed to counter the negative attitudes. I don't like to be around negative people.

YOSHI: Why?

PATRICK; For one thing, they depress me and bring me down. They also have a tendency to be nay-sayers instead of yea-sayers. I want to be around people who are positive and bring me up.

YOSHI: It certainly makes life more pleasant when you surround yourself with people who are positive and encouraging instead of discouraging.

PATRICK: That's something I noticed about you that you are a very positive person.

YOSHI: I wasn't always like that. Many times I fell into the woe-is-me trap. I liked to have a pity party until I realized that I was in control of my own destiny and that whining would never change anything. I had the power to change my life for the better. Once I changed my attitude, I changed my life.

PATRICK: I heard someone once say that your attitude measures your altitude. You can go as high in life as you want if you have the right attitude.

YOSHI: We could even apply that to Superman as he could fly pretty high.

PATRICK: You are really trying to convince me that we have super powers even to fly.

YOSHI: You just said that if you have the right attitude, you can soar like an eagle or like superman.

PATRICK: Okay, you win. We do have powers which if applied in the right way, can be super.

76

YOSHI: Thomas Macaulay said that the measure of a man's real character is what he would do if he knew he would never be found out.

PATRICK: That is a heavy thought. I heard a similar saying that character is what you do when no one is watching.

YOSHI: It's like people who have a public persona and a private persona. They should be the same. I think the people we admire most are often termed 'real' because they do not pretend to be something they are not.

PATRICK: Don't we hold some people to higher standards and expect them to be better than us?

YOSHI: Give me an example.

PATRICK: Sports figures for example. Kids seem to admire stars in any sport but sometimes they disappoint because they do something that causes us to face the fact that they are human.

YOSHI: Going back to Superman again, we know he was not human but his human persona, Clark Kent, was very much like us having traits that we could identify with such as being clumsy around Lois Lane. We do have a tendency to put certain public figures on a pedestal, but we have to remember that no one is perfect.

PATRICK: We only see their public persona and don't know what they do in private which means we don't know their true character.

YOSHI: Good point. You are right in that we have to judge them on how they act in public.

PATRICK: We use the term hypocrite when we talk about people who preach one thing and then do the opposite.

YOSHI: The origin of the word is from the Latin meaning a stage actor or pretender.

PATRICK: Shakespeare said it right that the whole world is a stage and we just actors.

YOSHI: So are we inferring that a person's character is based on how one acts?

PATRICK: Well, actions do tell us something about the person but for me someone's true character is revealed by both words and actions and how someone lives his/her life.

YOSHI: So is character based on external signs?

PATRICK: No, there has to be some intangibles there that we can't see.

YOSHI: So we can't really judge a person's character because all we have to judge is what we can see.

PATRICK: I think we can get a hint of a person's true character by his/her actions but we don't know things like motivation-why they do what they do.

YOSHI: Good point. For example, there are people we admire because they give a lot of money to worthy causes, but it may be just for the tax benefits.

PATRICK: Yes, true. I think we use the term ulterior motive to describe such an example.

YOSHI: Do we admire them less for that?

PATRICK: No, because we rarely know their motive. For me, it is person who donates his/her time and skills to a cause that is the true hero.

YOSHI: There is a tendency to "throw money" at a problem which many times does not solve the problem. I am with you in that giving of yourself is a better indication of a person's motive. Going back to Superman, he always acted personally to help people. He used his powers for good.

PATRICK: But there was Lex Luther who was there to oppose and undermine him.

YOSHI: He is a symbol of those who try to destroy our character. Too many people take pleasure in bringing someone down especially if they are in public life. Why do you think that is?

PATRICK: It could be due to one of those deadly sins-envy. They want to be the hero, get all the glory.

YOSHI: Dante defined this as 'a desire to deprive other men of theirs.'

PATRICK: So character is continuing to do what is right despite the fact that there are those who will try stand in your way.

YOSHI: I think that is a good definition. We talked about people in public life and the importance of what we refer to as reputation. This is what William Hersey David said in his poem "Reputation and Character:"

> *The circumstances amid which you love determine your reputation; the truth you believe determines your character.*
>
> *Reputation is what you are supposed to be; character is what you are.*
>
> *Reputation is the photograph; character is the face.*
>
> *Reputation comes over one from without; character grows up from within.*
>
> *Reputation is what you have when you come to a new community; character is what you have when you go away.*
>
> *Your reputation is learned in an hour; your character does not come to light for a year.*
>
> *Reputation is made in a moment; character is built in a life time.*
>
> *Reputation grows like a mushroom; character grows like the oak.*

*A single newspaper report gives you your reputation;
a life of toil gives you your character.*

*Reputation makes you rich or makes you poor;
character makes you happy or makes you miserable.*

*Reputation is what men say about you on your
tombstone; character is what angels say about you
before the throne of God.*

PATRICK: That is a lot to think about.

YOSHI: But it is important to think about character. What would you like written on your tombstone?

PATRICK: That I made a difference and left the world a better place than when I entered it.

YOSHI: Admirable sentiment but now the challenge is what do you do so that you deserve that on your tombstone?

PATRICK: I think that is for another day. Stay well, Yoshi. See you soon.

YOSHI: I look forward to our next discussion.

Yoshi's Yardsticks for Success:
What character traits do you admire in a person? List them below. Is there something you can do to strengthen your own character? Set a goal in that direction.

_____

_____

_____

_____

Thought of the day:
      "It is not what he has, nor even what he does, which directly expresses the worth of a man, but what he is."
                                    Henri Frederic Amiel

Seed 10. A First-Rate Education Serves You Well in Life

THE SCENE:

It is a rainy day in Los Angeles with the El Nino making its presence felt. Patrick invites Yoshi to his small apartment in the Wilshire District.

PATRICK: Welcome, Yoshi. Would you like some hot tea?

YOSHI: Yes, thank you. It is good for a cold, rainy day. (He walks around the small living room and stops at a framed poem which he reads aloud.)

> THE BUILDER
>
> A builder built a temple,
> He wrought it with grace and skill;
> Pillars and groins and arches
> All fashioned to work his will.
> Men said, as they saw its beauty,
> "It shall never know decay;
> Great is thy skill, O Builder!
> Thy fame shall endure for aye."
>
> A Teacher built a temple
> With loving and infinite care,
> Planning each arch with patience,
> Laying each stone with prayer.
> None praised her unceasing efforts,
> None knew of her wondrous plan,

For the temple the Teacher built
Was unseen by the eyes of man.
Gone is the Builder's temple,
Crumpled into the dust;
Low lies each stately pillar,
Food for consuming rust.
But the temple the Teacher built
Will last while the ages roll,
For that beautiful unseen temple
Was a child's immortal soul.

PATRICK: I found that at a swap meet and read it often.

YOSHI: The line that strikes me is that of it being unseen by the eyes of man. Sometimes we only put our trust in what we can see, but the impact we make on people can't be seen.

PATRICK: I often hear kids say that they don't see the importance of learning a subject such as history. They don't think that events that happened two hundred years ago have relevance today.

YOSHI: Santayana is often quoted about those not learning from history are destined to repeat it, but there is another quote that has to do with education. He said that the great difficulty in education is to get experience out of ideas.

PATRICK: I used to complain about learning Latin. I knew that the old Mass was in Latin but with English now being the norm, I thought studying Latin was a waste, but I discovered something later in life.

YOSHI: Hindsight is 20/20 as they say.

PATRICK: Yes, true. Now that I am studying Spanish, I find my Latin is valuable. It is the basis of the Romance Languages so it will help make learning easier.

YOSHI: I think the schools need to do a better job of making learning relevant to life and the real world.

PATRICK: Going back to the poem, teachers are building a temple, laying the foundation for a successful life.

YOSHI: I still go back it being unseen. I think that has two meanings: the impact teachers make on students and their not seeing the relevance of education.

PATRICK: It reminds me of the arguments about whether a classical education is worthwhile. In the seminary I read classics in the original languages such as Caesar's Gallic Wars in Latin and Wilhelm Tell in German. It was agonizing for me translating the passages. At the time I hated it, but now I appreciate having had the experience. Has it helped me in life? I could say it has had no effect on my life that I can tell but then again, I appreciate the classics more and it gave me confidence in my ability to meet the challenge so those were some positive effects.

YOSHI: Plus it helps when playing Jeopardy.

PATRICK: (laughing) Yes, it does.

YOSHI: So far we have talked about book learning, but I am sure the education you received was more than what came out of the books you studied.

PATRICK: That is for sure. My seminary education was also about forming the person, my character. It also shaped my values.

YOSHI: So a good education involves not only knowledge of the world but of self. It goes back to the admonition of the Greeks who said to know thyself.

PATRICK: I like the line out of Shakespeare that goes "to thine own self be true and it must follow as night follows day thou can't be false to any man."

YOSHI: If my memory serves me right that is part of the soliloquy of Polonius to his son who is going off to college.

PATRICK: Yes, that was a father giving his some good advice. There were some other memorable words of wisdom in that speech. Let me Google it. Here it is. (Reads aloud.)

> Lord Polonious: Yet there, Laertes! Aboard, aboard, for shame! The wind sits in the shoulder of your sail, and you are stay'd for. There; my blessing with thee

and these few precepts in thy memory. See thou character. Give thy thoughts no tongue, nor any unproportioned thought his act. Be thou familiar, but by no means vulgar. Those friends thou hast, and their adoption tried, grapple them to thy soul with hoops of steel; but do not dull thy palm with entertainment of each new-hatch'd, unfledged comrade. Beware of entrance to a quarrel, but being in, bear't that the opposed may beware of thee. Give every man they ear, but few thy voice; take each man's censure, but reserve thy judgment. Costly thy habit as thy purse can buy, but not express'd in fancy; rich, not gaudy; for the apparel oft proclaims the man, and they in France of the best rank and station are of a most select and generous chief in that. Neither a borrower nor a lender be; for loan oft loses both itself and friend, and borrowing dulls the edge of husbandry. This above all: to thine ownself be true, and it must follow, as the night the day, Thou canst not then be false to any man. Farewell: my blessing season this in thee!

YOSHI: There is so much in there to think about, and Polonius seemed to understand that his son's college education was about more than book knowledge because he starts off talking about character.

PATRICK: He told his son to think before he speaks. How many relationships have been ruined by people blurting out their thoughts before thinking about the consequences of their words?

YOSHI: I think his advice about friends was very important. I once heard a great speaker, Charlie Tremendous Jones, say that your life in five years will be the result of the books you read and the friends you have around you.

PATRICK: I am happy that I found out early in life that friends influence you more than you care to admit. In the seminary we were encouraged to have multiple friends and not just one or two. In those formative teen years, the friends make a huge impact on your life because we are all trying to find ourselves and look to others for guidance.

YOSHI: How about his admonition that the apparel often proclaims the man. Polonious is making the case that people will judge you by your appearance.

PATRICK: I never had to worry about that in the seminary because we wore black cassocks but now I do pay attention to what I wear.

YOSHI: I wish more people did. In California we tend to dress more casually but sometimes too much so. We preach not to prejudge someone, but it is difficult to not have an opinion about someone who does not dress well or lacks good hygiene.

PATRICK: I like the fact that more schools are returning to uniforms. I went into a school recently to apply for a teaching position and was taken back by the number of t-shirts that to me had inappropriate pictures or language. I think education should also include proper manners and social skills.

YOSHI: I hear that etiquette classes are in great demand now.

PATRICK: That should be a part of the school curriculum. It would help these young people in life and also raise their own self-esteem.

YOSHI: How so?

PATRICK: By giving them the confidence in being able to be comfortable in social situations. Young people mostly go to fast food restaurants but are like fish out of water if they have to go into a sit down restaurant that has more than one fork.

YOSHI: Good point. There is another area of education that needs to be added to the curriculum and that is money handling. Remember what Polonius said to his son about borrowing and lending money. It was a good way to lose friends but to me ignorance of money management is far worse.

PATRICK: I never learned how to balance a checkbook, but we did have math problems dealing with interest on money earned. It is amazing the kids today have credit cards. I wonder if they truly understand how to use them wisely.

YOSHI: I doubt if Polonius would have let his son have one because he would know that it would lead to his financial ruin. Most young people don't have the restraint to control their spending.

PATRICK: I never really had to worry about money in the seminary as everything was provided us so I was not prepared when I went out into the world to handle my expenses.

YOSHI: How did you do it?

PATRICK: I had to sit down and figure out how to balance my income and expenses. I knew exactly how much I had to buy food after paying rent and utilities. I was able to balance my budget.

YOSHI: Maybe you should run for governor.

PATRICK: (laughing) I am sure my budget is manageable compared to the State of California. On the surface it seems so simple, spend less than you take in but with the world's eighth largest economy, not so simple.

YOSHI: But if we taught that in our schools, maybe we would have fewer bankruptcies and home foreclosures. We need to do the math and see how it can make our life better.

PATRICK: Thinking about my seminary education, I did learn valuable lessons about life as far as living a spiritual life but not so much the secular. In the long run, it is the spiritual I needed more at that time in my life.

YOSHI: Yes, and now you are learning the other side-survival and it is the spiritual side that will help you navigate the pitfalls of life and keep you on the right path.

PATRICK: I have no regrets about the education I received because I know that whatever is thrown at me, I can handle it with confidence.

YOSHI: The rain has stopped and now I can head to the gardens. Stay well, my friend.

PATRICK: You too and see you soon.

Yoshi's Yardsticks for Success:
Think about your education and write down two subjects you learned and how you can use them to make your life better.

_____
_____
_____
_____
_____
_____
_____
_____
_____
_____
_____
_____

Thought of the day:
"Education does not mean teaching people to know what they do not know; it means teaching them to behave as they do not behave."
John Ruskin

Seed 11. Advisors and Mentors...Follow the Leaders

THE SCENE:

Patrick is at the Huntington Gardens late on a Friday hoping to catch Yoshi before he leaves work. He finds the man in the tool shed cleaning and arranging all the gardening equipment. Patrick knocks on the door and is welcomed by Yoshi.

YOSHI: Hi, Patrick. You have come late in the day, not your usual schedule.

PATRICK: I was out pounding the pavement looking for work.

YOSHI: Any luck?

PATRICK: Not yet, but I am confident I will find a job soon. Schools will be hiring for the new school year and maybe I can even get into summer school. (noticing in the large array of tools and plants). How did you ever learn about all the tools and plants?

YOSHI: I had a mentor whom I followed around for years. He was a master gardener in Japan and took me under his wing when I was a teen. I loved plants and being outside. I had watched my father tend his garden and helped there too, but it wasn't until high school that I met the teacher who really got me interested in working with plants.

PATRICK: You were very fortunate to have someone to guide you.

YOSHI: You must have had people in your life who gave you direction.

PATRICK: Yes, at a young age I had a cousin, Father Leon Loranger, a Jesuit priest who often counseled me on behavior and planted the seeds that would later inspire me to enter the seminary.

YOSHI: It is so important, especially at an early age, to have someone that can keep you on the right path. It is too easy to drift off into territory that can lead to bad behavior.

PATRICK: You are right about that. In grade school I had priests and nuns who seemed to recognize something in me that was special and who influenced me greatly. Sometimes I was made fun of and called a "goodie-two-shoes" but I didn't care about that. In my heart, I was happy to have their guidance.

YOSHI: In the seminary you must have had counselors.

PATRICK: We had a Jesuit spiritual advisor who met with us on a regular basis. Our high school counselor was pretty straight laced. I remember how shy he was when talking about sex. He used to look down and seemed to be embarrassed, but he had to discuss the subject. We were one hundred teen-aged boys with normal hormones like any other boys.

YOSHI: If this is uncomfortable for you, you don't have to discuss this.

PATRICK: No, it's okay. At the time, I was very innocent and really didn't know much but when I got to the college, our Jesuit spiritual advisor had a very different approach. He had been chaplain at Cook County Hospital in Chicago and to say he was a man of the world is an understatement.

YOSHI: How so?

PATRICK: He was very direct and open in talking about a variety of subjects including sex. I am sure he had dealt with everything sexual in the big city. We were fascinated by his stories. He felt that as priests we had to be prepared to deal with many situations. He wanted us to realize that although we were to be representatives of Christ, we were still human and had feelings and emotions.

YOSHI: It sounds like he was preparing you to go out into the real world which was very different from the sheltered world where you spent most of the time.

PATRICK: I got a taste of that world during the summer when I went home for vacation. There was a mentor there for me too.

YOSHI: Who was that?

PATRICK: It was my parish priest who recommended me to the Bishop as a candidate for the seminary. He was there for me and made sure I continued on the spiritual path by attending regular Mass, going to confession, and participating in church activities.

YOSHI: So you were still in a sheltered environment even when you were home.

PATRICK: Yes, but I was also in a situation where I was exposed to the temptations of the world.

YOSHI: How so?

PATRICK: I had a summer job working the snack bar at the country club which was part of the company my mother worked for. It was on the lake and I had to interact with kids my age who were not so holy, if you know what I mean.

YOSHI: That had to be difficult for a young teenage boy who was committed to the spiritual and not the temporal.

PATRICK: Yes, there was an element there that made me attractive to the girls. I think it had to do with seeing me as a challenge.

YOSHI: To see if they could lead you off the straight and narrow, so to speak.

PATRICK: They did tease me both verbally and physically.

YOSHI: How did you fend off their advances, if you don't mind me asking.

PATRICK: I had a screen between myself and the customers which served as a barrier. I was pretty much committed to my goal of becoming a priest, but I think it was good for me to be tempted.

YOSHI: It was a test of your resolve. Remember, Jesus was tempted when he was out in the desert.

PATRICK: I kept that focus for four years but once in college, I started to think differently.

YOSHI: What did you mentor say about all this?

PATRICK: His cure-all was prayer and to avoid putting myself into situations that would lead to sin.

YOSHI: That would have meant giving up your summer job.

PATRICK: I couldn't to that. The job helped me pay for my expenses at the seminary. I suppose I could have found another job, but I felt I could handle it.

YOSHI: I am sure you seminary training gave you the strength to prevail.

PATRICK: Yes, and the fact that I had someone I could talk to.

YOSHI: Did you have a mentor after you left the seminary?

PATRICK: I did have a counselor at the college who helped me navigate the courses and recommend a career path for me.

YOSHI: That must have been a difficult transition from a seminary college to a secular college.

PATRICK: I had my courses all chosen for me in the seminary but when I got to the university, I had to choose my own but having a career goal helped me make my experience both worthwhile and fulfilling. I had the discipline to manage my time well which to me is a major element in success in college.

YOSHI: Not to mention in life. Did you ever hear of a television show called "Meeting of the Minds"?

PATRICK: No. What was it about?

YOSHI: It was hosted by Steve Allen who created the Tonight Show. The show had characters from history meet and discuss their lives, times, and philosophies. I remember an exchange between Attila the Hun and Cleopatra. It was a fascinating exchange and brilliantly done. Using the concept, if you gather a roundtable of mentors, who would you invite?

PATRICK: That is an intriguing idea. Could I choose anyone?

YOSHI: Yes, living or dead. You must have reason for your choice so think carefully.

PATRICK: I'd like to hear your choices too. First of all, I would invite Jesus Christ because His teachings so influenced thought that His advice would make Him the perfect mentor who lived what He taught. How about you?

YOSHI: I would choose Buddha for the same reason.

PATRICK: Another person I would like at my table is Henry David Thoreau. I have read <u>Walden</u> many times and his chapters on economy, sounds and solitude still resonate. He was one of the first environmentalists who listened to the wildlife and respected it.

YOSHI: Since you picked a literary mentor, I would choose Lao Tzu. He is the author of The *Daodejing*, often called simply *the Laozi* after its reputed author, which describes the Dao (or Tao) as the mystical source and ideal of all existence: it is unseen, but not transcendent, immensely powerful yet supremely humble, being the root of all things. According to the *Daodejing*, humans have no special place within the Dao, being just one of its many ("ten thousand") manifestations. People have desires and free will (and thus are able to alter their own nature). Many act "unnaturally", upsetting the natural balance of the Dao. The *Daodejing* intends to lead students to a "return" to their natural state, in harmony with Dao.

PATRICK: I think that is a good description of what Thoreau was also trying to convey that we should return to our natural state.

YOSHI: Who else would you invite to your mentor roundtable?

PATRICK: I would want to talk and learn from John F. Kennedy especially for his courage during the Cuban Missile Crisis and for the brain trust he surrounded himself with. He had a great mind and was an inspiration.

YOSHI: In the same vein, I would choose Winston Churchill who was a great statesman and who also displayed courage under fire during the bombing of London during WWII. He too inspired especially at a time when the Brits were being hammered by Hitler.

PATRICK: I need to read more about Churchill. I want to keep my group diverse so I would invite someone from the arts. I would want to probe the mind of William Shakespeare. His plays were full of wisdom. We talked about the famous speech by Polonius whose son was going off to college. There are so many great soliloquies.

YOSHI: Good choice. If I had to choose someone from the arts, I would like to sit down with Mark Twain not only for his wit but his insightful observations about life and politics.

PATRICK: I would round out my group with someone who is considered a motivator such as Dale Carnegie. I read his famous book How to Win Friends and Influence People at an early age and it influenced my life greatly.

YOSHI: I would choose The Power of Positive Thinking by Norman Vincent Peale which made me look at life from a very different perspective.

PATRICK: I think we would have quite an interesting panel of minds. It would be fascinating to hear them interact. I am going to make a list of books to read over the next few months that will lift me and inspire me to pursue my goals.

YOSHI: So our conclusion is that not only people can mentor you but books can be a source of wisdom too.

PATRICK: Yes, for the times when you can't interact face to face, books can fill the void.

YOSHI: You have inspired me to update my reading list. Time to head home. I'll lock up and walk you to your car.

PATRICK: It's been a pleasure exploring our mentors. Let's meet again soon.

Yoshi's Yardsticks for Success:
Consider mentors you had in life and write down how they influenced you.

Is there someone you can mentor? Who would you invite to your mentor roundtable?

_____
_____
_____
_____
_____
_____
_____
_____
_____
_____
_____
_____
_____

Thought of the day:

INFLUENCE

Drop a pebble in the water,
And its ripples reach out far;
And the sunbeams dancing on them
May reflect them to a star.

Give a smile to someone passing,
Thereby making his morning glad,
It may greet you in the evening
When your own heart may be sad.

Do a deed of simple kindness;
Though its end you may not see,
It may reach, like widening ripples,
Down a long eternity.

Joseph Norris

Seed 12. Hindsight and Foresight

THE SCENE:

Patrick is driving down the 405 Freeway again listening to Cat Stevens CD <u>Tea for the Tillerman</u> but this time when the track "On the Road to Find Out" begins, his thoughts are not of wondering where he is going but where he has been.

Months ago at the Huntington Botanical Gardens he met Yoshi who became his sounding board, his ear and advisor who helped lead him to where he would find out what he wanted in life.

He thinks about all the subjects they had discussed over the months. Patrick had come to the realization that what he had learned in the seminary, all those seeds that were planted, would now come to fruition. He had indeed been nurtured by the experience, so much so, that now he was sure of what he wanted to do with his life.

After he reached home, he called Yoshi.

PATRICK: Hi Yoshi. It's Patrick.

YOSHI: Patrick, it is good to hear from you.

PATRICK: I apologize for not coming by lately but I have been out arranging my travel.

YOSHI: So you decided to take off for parts unknown?

PATRICK: No actually, I do know where I am going and thanks to you, I have an idea how I can put that seminary education to good use.

YOSHI: So our talks did help you.

PATRICK: Very much. When I first approached you, I was unsure of what to do with my life but more importantly how to put my seminary education to good use. My first thought was about teaching, but I realized that if I began a full-time job, I would not get a chance to get out and see the world.

YOSHI: You discovered in our conversations that you had led a very sheltered life.

PATRICK: Yes, I realized that and something I wanted to rectify. I needed to get out there and experience what the world has to offer.

YOSHI: You are still young, Patrick, and have plenty of time to settle down.

PATRICK: True, and I didn't want to have any regrets later in life that I didn't take the opportunity when it presented itself.

YOSHI: What opportunity is that?

PATRICK: To enlist in the military.

YOSHI: Which branch?

PATRICK: The U.S. Air Force.

YOSHI: Why that one?

PATRICK: My uncles were both in the Air Force, and I got a great offer that allowed me to use that seminary experience, specifically languages.

YOSHI: I remember that you had six years of Latin and five years of German.

PATRICK: Right and when I took the battery of tests, they found I had an aptitude for languages so I am off to Monterey, California after basic training.

YOSHI: What is in Monterey?

PATRICK: The Defense Language Institute where I will be studying Indonesian.

YOSHI: Why that language?

PATRICK: It seems that with the rise of terrorist groups, our government may need some linguists.

YOSHI: That sounds very interesting and the experience could open doors for you into various diplomatic channels.

PATRICK: I hadn't thought about that but you are right.

YOSHI: If you have been following the news closely, the United States is engaged throughout the world, and there is a need for linguists.

PATRICK: I am aware of that. I decided to take the initiative and see what opportunities were out there.

YOSHI: That is a good example of being proactive and going for what you want not letting someone else decide for you.

PATRICK: I am a firm believer that things happen for a reason as well as the people we meet. I know now that I was meant to meet you.

YOSHI: I think there is something to that. Remember I met someone who changed my life and led me to my current profession.

PATRICK: I will be looking for someone in the military who can mentor me. It will be a big change for me. The military life is so different from the seminary life.

YOSHI: True but the very principles you learned in the seminary can help you succeed in the military. Think back to all the positive traits you acquired and I am sure you can apply them to any career because they are principles of success.

PATRICK: You are right, Yoshi. I am confident I have what it takes to be successful no matter what career I choose.

YOSHI: One last thing, Patrick. Don't give up on your original choice-being a teacher. I feel that you have so much to offer there.

PATRICK: I will use my military experience to further my own education but also prepare me better for the teaching profession.

YOSHI: Then you are on the right path. You must keep me informed of your progress. I am sure you will have a very interesting assignment after language school.

PATRICK: I have no idea what I am going to do with the language, but I am eager to find out.

YOSHI: You are on the road to find out again.

PATRICK: (laughing) Cat Stevens keeps coming back to me.

YOSHI: It seems music continues to have meaning in our lives. You had mentioned that song many times so it must have a deep personal message for you.

PATRICK: It certainly does. There is a line in the song that says that there is so much left to know and that the answer lies within and to take a look now.

YOSHI: And kick out the devil's sin, pick up, pick up the Good Book now.

PATRICK: Yoshi, you surprise me. How did you know the rest of the lyric?

YOSHI: I listen and I learn. You don't think I was learning from you too?

PATRICK: *Touche!* Good advice about picking up the Good Book. I plan on doing that a lot. I promise to keep in touch and send you postcards from exotic places.

YOSHI: I look forward to it, my friend. You know where to find me. God's speed!

PATRICK: Thanks, Yoshi and keep caring for the gardens. Goodbye.

Yoshi's Yardsticks for Success:
Take a look at your past. What did you learn and how can you apply it to make your life better?

_____
_____
_____
_____
_____
_____
_____
_____
_____
_____
_____

Thought of the day:

From RABBI BEN EZRA

Grow old along with me!
The best is yet to be,
The last of life, for which the first was made:
Our times are in his hand
Who saith, "A whole I planned,
Youth shows but half; trust God:
See all, nor be afraid!"

Robert Browning

w Patrick's career in the next book- The Military Seeds: Life's
s Learned in Military Service.

About the Author

Frank Barry has been an educator for over 30 years and often gives credit to his seminary education for his success in life. The Latin and German languages he learned in the seminary led him to become a linguist for the U.S. Air Force having studied the Indonesian, Vietnamese, and Hebrew languages. He completed his degree at the University of Massachusetts in Boston and obtained his teaching credential.

He has been an English teacher, school administrator, and is currently teaching part time as a Vocational English as a Second Language instructor in companies throughout Southern California.

He lives in Huntington Beach, California and enjoys his volunteer work with the Kiwanis and with high school Key Clubs in service to the community. He is Economic Opportunities Chair for the Vietnam Veterans of America.

He is currently at work on the second book in the Seed Series-The Military Seeds and is completing a screenplay-"Bridge to Boyle Heights" about his teaching experience and cultural awakening in East Los Angeles.

…ion can be obtained at www.ICGtesting.com

'13

001B/1/P

Overcoming The Seduction Of Disloyalty

Jezebel, Go To Hell!

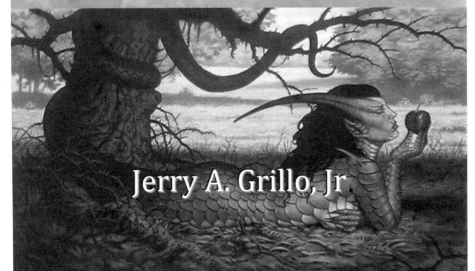

Jerry A. Grillo, Jr

FZM Publishing
Copyright 2009
"Overcoming The Seduction Of Disloyalty"
By Fogzone Ministries
P.O. Box 3707 Hickory, NC. 28603

Second Print
2010

All rights reserved under International Copyright Law. Contents and/or cover may not be reproduced in whole or in part in any form without the express written consent of the publisher.

All Scriptures, unless indicated, are taken from the King James Version

Scriptures quotations marked NJKV are taken from the New King James Version

Scriptures quotations marked NIV are taken from the New International Version.

ISBN
978-1-4276-3986-8

Printed in the United States of America

Special Thanks

*F*irst, I want to thank my wonderful family. Maryann, you are the best wife any man could have. Your wisdom and counsel are golden. My two children, Jerry III and Jordan; there are no human words to describe how much I love you. You three make my life worth living every single day.

April Mercer, your dedication and loyalty to helping advance these projects to completion is truly appreciated. I know those who are blessed by these books are very grateful for your dedication and hard work... Your input and changes are an incredible help.

I want to thank each of my proofreaders. Thank you for your love and support. You are wonderful proofreaders, and I know you will write your own books in the future.

FZ Design -your graphic work and friendship help make every project a joy.

To all my partners who sow money and time into my ministry; especially those who are members at The Favor Center. Thank you so much for your love and confidence in allowing me to do what I do.

To my parents, you are the greatest... Love spending time with you. Your prayers are very important. Also, to my second set of parents-some call them "in-laws," I call them family.

Table of Contents

ENDORSEMENTS

The spirit of Jezebel is cancerous, contagious and deadly to the vision of every spiritual leader. It is like a snake whose head is hidden and almost impossible to find... Every Leader must read this book. Believe it. Keep it on your desk for the next 90 days.
   Dr. Mike Murdock
   The Wisdom Center
   Dallas, TX

We are truly living in the days of the Prophet Elijah! Idol worship, brutal slaughtering of unborn babies; the seductive **"Spirit of Jezebel"** is running rapid throughout the land! On the other hand, God is pouring out a fresh, dynamic anointing on His chosen people that will force the Jezebel spirit back to hell!

I was in the first live service when this message was methodically delivered from Bishop Jerry Grillo. I trembled as I realized the eternal implications to the Church if this spirit was permitted to continue to operate uncontested. And now, before the ink has dried on the final manuscript, I have read the book, "Jezebel, Go To Hell!"

God has not forgotten His people! In times past God has always raised up a person and anointed them with a breakthrough anointing; a divine messenger for His people for such a time as this. Bishop Grillo is one of those God-called and anointed men. Masterfully written. Strategically outlined. Provocatively energizing. This book offers it's searching reader a Biblical compass to Jezebel's cunning deception and relentless tactics to control... uncovering her primary goal to decapitate spiritual leadership and authority like a careful surgeon. This book is a

must read for every believer who is ready to join forces together with Bishop Grillo and me shouting with one accord, "Jezebel, Go To Hell!" Your Spiritual Life Will Never Be The Same!
Dr. Todd Coontz
RockWealth Ministries
Aiken, SC

Along with the "Men of Honor" at my church, we agree that the lesson, "The Secrets to Loyalty" Dr. Grillo taught was on point and revolutionized my church. I've never seen that many men cry out like spanked babies as the Lord used Dr. Grillo to penetrate our hearts the way he did.

Dr. Grillo asked the question: **"Are you a predator or a partner?"**—and silence permeated throughout the whole sanctuary because each man was searching his heart to see if he was one, or the other.

Dr. Grillo enlightened and taught us about the **five different Insurrectionists**: Lucifer, Absalom, Jezebel, Ahab and Judas. We were all glued to his presentation as he explained and spoke about the **Stages of Disloyalty**, Witchcraft and Rebellion, and **Signs of Disloyalty**.

When the altar call was made, I saw, what seemed like a herd of cattle rushing to a water hole because of their dire need of thirst. Before the words came out of Dr. Grillo's mouth to come to the altar, the altar was full to its capacity.

Like us, you are guaranteed to be blessed and moved to a new dimension. Don't just take my word for it—receive this insightful wisdom on, **"Jezebel Go To Hell!"**
Bishop Harvey Bee
Christian Fellowship Church
Warner Robins, GA

Bishop Grillo is fast becoming a leading voice of authority regarding different spirits within the church.

Having him minister at our Emotional Healing Conference became a valuable training session to our leadership and a needed breakthrough to many of our members.

To say that Bishop Grillo is qualified to pen these pages would be an understatement. To leave this book unread would be a mistake. You hold in your hand a key to unlocking the life that God desires for you. I dare you to turn these pages with even the least little bit of expectation and watch as God begins to show out in your life!

> Bishop Jeff Poole
> New Hope International
> Warner Robins, GA

The Spirit of Disloyalty is a silent force holding back the church from walking in the power and purpose of God... In this book, Dr. Grillo exposes masterfully the spirit of the Jezebel's influence and equips the body of Christ to deal with and cast it out of your life FOREVER so we can reign in the Kingdom of God. I highly recommend this book.

> Pastor Tyronne Stowe
> Former NFL Linebacker
> Gospel 4 Life Church
> Phoenix AZ

Introduction

$\mathcal{W}$rong people in our lives can create wrong seasons in our lives.

To avoid frustration and delayed harvests we must discern whom we are allowing to hang around us, to work for us and know our secrets. I've learned that I am not obligated to change a deceiver around me. However, I am obligated to discern a deceiver and move swiftly away from them.

"Discernment is when your spirit is telling you something your mind isn't."

When we begin to discern people, we will begin to better equip our lives to be protected from those who are sent by the enemy to tear us down... to destroy our vision... to weaken our focus and break our spirit, creating in us a season of depression, dissension and discouragement. Wrong people are the enemy's number one focus breaker. The devil doesn't destroy ministries. People do! Pastors who get caught up in wrong living destroy their ministry. Sheep who give their ear to wrong voices and wrong thinking begin to become disloyal. They hurt the church or the ministry in the end.

I believe one of the reasons there are so many relationship splits, church splits and ministry wars, is because wrong people have been left uncorrected... uncontested... They are not confronted in time to stop the problem. These people have wormed their way in, not to promote ministry, or the name of Jesus, but to promote their own agenda and control what's going on in our churches.

In this book, we will learn about the five insurrectionist personalities and how we, as leaders, can defeat them and throw them out of our lives.

I've titled this book "Jezebel Go To Hell" because she is the most known of the five insurrectionists. This book is a study about all five and also how to overcome and recognize disloyalty. I heard a quote the other day that fits this manuscript, "If we don't have loyalty we are no better than the beast at the door." If we don't teach and practice loyalty in our leadership and in our church families then we are no better than the beast at our doors.

Let me clue you in. This spirit is not trying to stand behind the pulpit or sit in the position of a leader. Its goal is to control the pulpit, or leader, from behind the scenes. This is why these disloyal subjects are compared to a serpent. Their serpent-like attitude goes unnoticed for so long that when these insurrectionists are finally exposed to leadership the venom of their bite has now infected a part, if not the entire body of the local assembly.

There is only one way to deal with these guys. They must be exposed quickly. They must be dealt with swiftly, and they must be either placed under supervision and restored or asked to leave the local house.

The way you deal with a snake is to cut off its head. I am aware that this sounds so fierce and unloving but let me inform you I've yet to know anyone who has conquered the Jezebel spirit in a way that causes them to be restored and placed back in submission to the leadership (not to say that it cannot happen). This book is how to deal with and notice these disloyal so called religious people.

This spirit, in my opinion, is unchangeable. This spirit is evil and beguiles people into a seduction of hatred and misconduct among those who were first walking in agreement with you. Dethrone this spirit quickly before it worms its way through those who are weak and feeling a dissatisfaction in your leadership, or congregation. Silence this voice swiftly! Make no treaty with it. JEZEBEL, GO TO HELL!

I have been holding this book in my spirit for a long time. Watching those in other churches deal with the false prophet and Jezebel spirit has angered me to rise up and declare war on this foul and evil spirit.

No more! It's time for us to stand up and be informed. We are not going to allow this spirit to reign and control our people any longer.

I have put together information that I have learned and experienced through the past twenty-five years of ministry. I do believe that this book is going to silence wrong voices around you.

WHOEVER HAS YOUR EAR HAS YOUR FUTURE!

Dr. Jerry A. Grillo, Jr.

Preface

$\mathscr{I}$ve read many books on the spirit of Jezebel and the spirits of insurrection that sit among the church each week. One great book is, "Confronting the Jezebel." In this book, I am not only going to expose the spirit of the Jezebel but the spirit of disloyalty.

When someone decides to become disloyal they enter into a spirit of rebellion. They become cynical and critical of what the **head leader** is doing and the direction the church is taking.

It is my goal to you five possible personalities that these disloyal people have. I will describe them to you and give you the solution on how to take care of them.

I believe the church is in need of a great healing. I can't tell you the times I've sat down to listen to the wounded in the House of God; not just sheep, but pastors, bishops and worship leaders. I have heard horror stories of how they were treated and belittled in the name of religion. My heart is angered at the lack of responsibility the "pew-sitter" has taken in this organization, or body, we call the church.

Never have we seen such hatred. Never have we witnessed such cold, calloused feelings as when we watch a person turning their heart away from their pastor. When they do, they first start with disconnecting from the whole of his teaching. They begin to ask questions about who their leader is, and if he really has any authority over them. As soon as someone begins to question the power and authority of their leader they have opened their minds for the spirit of disloyalty to step in and deceive them.

There may be more than five insurrectionists in the Bible, but I believe the five I discuss are the doors for all the others to walk through.

I have had to face every one of these enemies. They have

drained and wearied me to the point of wanting to leave the ministry. I have sat in my office and cried about those who I thought were "holy" and "called," but in the end I had to pull out their daggers of hate and anger. Let me help you; they don't leave quietly and in order. Expect pain and problems when they go. I tried for so long to pray this problem out or to hope it would just get up and leave. The truth is that you can't run from this problem. The only cure is through powerful partnership.

Elijah anointed three men to partner with him who became the deciding factor that destroyed those who were the enemy to the gospel and to God's man.

Hear me! Hear me clearly. You cannot win the battle over these insurrectionists without the power of the Holy Spirit and the willingness to confront. Running, bowing out, and even trying to work peace will not do. In the end, they will devour your spirit and take over your business, your ministry and even your church.

This spirit can even exist in your own immediate family. I know this for a fact. It is hard for parents to submit to one of their children if they are in headship. It is even harder for siblings to submit to one another. Trust me. The spirit of jealousy is always lurking in the corridor of their minds. If you find yourself serving your brother or sister, who is sitting in the seat of headship, make sure you guard your mind and most of all, guard your ears. It will be through this venue that the spirit of jealousy and envy will enter.

Miriam's Disloyalty

Look at Miriam, the sister of Moses. She was so excited to be leaving Egypt. She was even called a prophetess in Exodus:

"Then Miriam the prophetess, the sister of Aaron, took the timbrel in her hand; and all the women went out after her with timbrels and with dances. And Miriam answered them:"Sing to the Lord, For He has triumphed gloriously! The horse and its

rider He has thrown into the sea!" Exodus 15:20-21NKJV

It was easy for Miriam and Aaron to praise while everything was going well in the ministry of Moses. Success keeps the spirit of disloyalty silent. The demon that rises up against leadership won't show its face while there is success in the atmosphere. People usually won't listen to negative voices while the ship is making good head-way in troubled times.

Watch out when the waters start calming, and the wind of progress begins to fade. This is the climate and atmosphere that the spirit of the Jezebel will shine in.

"Then Miriam and Aaron spoke against Moses because of the Ethiopian woman whom he had married; for he had married an Ethiopian woman. So they said, "Has the Lord indeed spoken only through Moses? Has He not spoken through us also?" And the Lord heard it. (Now the man Moses was very humble, more than all men who were on the face of the earth.)?" Numbers 12:1-3 NKJV

Times had slowed down and the journey was becoming long and tiresome. People were starting to complain. They were becoming disgruntled, hungry, tired and questioning the ability of their leader. Here came the first attack. It didn't come from some foreigner or someone in the congregation. It showed up in Moses' own family; those who were close to him; his brother and sister.

Sometimes it's hard for family members to stay loyal and submitted. They have the privilege of getting to see the leader in relaxed times; they were there during childhood when the leader was seemingly a "nobody." They know their shortcomings. Family members must discern the distinction between the man or woman who is family and the man or woman who is anointed by God to be headship in the body of Christ.

Family members who choose to stay connected will have to fight some very serious spirits in their own minds.

Remember, it is impossible for the head to always wear the hat of a leader while resting and spending time with their family.

I've heard it said with sarcasm more than once from family members, *"You're supposed to be a pastor."*

Look what Miriam said to Aaron. ***"Has the Lord indeed spoken only through Moses? Has He not spoken through us also?"*** Wow! Here's trouble starting in a big way.

The mind of disloyalty has started. Yes, God does speak to others in our church. Yes, we all have a personal walk and relationship with the Lord, but when it comes to the corporate flow... the corporate anointing, when it involves the movement and growth of the whole body, you have lost your voice and your ear.

Don't think for a moment that God isn't still listening to what is being said at kitchen tables, restaurants and living rooms all over the city after church on Sunday. He's still got the back of his servants. ***"And the Lord heard it"*** *(Numbers 12:1:3).*

"Suddenly the Lord said to Moses, Aaron, and Miriam, "Come out, you three, to the tabernacle of meeting! Then the Lord came down in the pillar of cloud and stood in the door of the tabernacle, and called Aaron and Miriam. And they both went forward. Then He said,"Hear now My words: If there is a prophet among you, I, the Lord, make Myself known to him in a vision; I speak to him in a dream. Not so with My servant Moses; He is faithful in all My house. I speak with him face to face, Even plainly, and not in dark sayings; And he sees the form of the Lord. Why then were you not afraid To speak against My servant Moses?" Numbers 12:4-8 NKJV

The Lord was mad. He was so angry that He was ready to kill these people. He didn't care that they were related to Moses. They shouldn't have raised their voice against him in secret.

They would have been judged more severally if it hadn't been for Moses interceding on their behalf.

Family members must watch and guard their minds not to make the head in their family common when they have been selected by God to lead.

CLOSING THOUGHT

I believe that this book is going to help bring healing, commitment and change back to the local church and leadership. My goal is that it will also reestablish proper *order* and *government* in the church.

Use this book as a study to teach from. The first chapter is going to give you some history about Jezebel. Understanding the real "Jezebel" will help you see more clearly how this spirit has moved through the Bible, our churches, our businesses and anywhere there is someone who is in a main leadership role.

Let me caution you. This chapter is going to seem very deep, maybe even a little dry, but bear with it. Read it slowly. We are going to look at history's connection to Jezebel. We need to know her origin so we can find the root of seduction and disloyalty, and learn about the other insurrectionists and how they operate. This knowledge will help you discern them and stay far away from anyone who acts like them.

CHAPTER ONE

WHO IS JEZEBEL?

*J*ezebel was a queen of ancient Israel. Her story is told in 1st and 2nd *Kings*. She is introduced as a Phoenician princess, the daughter of King Ithobaal I, of Sidon, who marries King Ahab.

She turned Ahab away from the God of the Israelites and of the Jews (being the inhabitants of Judah in this context) and toward the worship of the Phoenician god, Baal. Ahab and Jezebel allowed temples of Baal to operate in Israel, and the pagan religion received royal patronage. Furthermore, the queen used her control over Ahab to lead the Hebrews into sin and subject them to tyranny. After she had the prophets of Yahweh slaughtered, the prophet Elijah challenged 450 prophets of Baal to a test (1 *Kings* 18), exposed their god as powerless and had *them* slaughtered.[i]

THE MEANING OF THE NAME:

Using the vowels traditionally used for the name "Jezebel" by Hebrew readers, the Hebrew form of this name means, **"not exalted,"** but it is highly unlikely her parents would have given her such a name. Read with different vowels it can be understood as meaning, **"Where is the Prince?"** In fact, early Syrian inscriptions from Ugarit demonstrate that **"The Prince"** (equivalent of Hebrew "Zebul") was a popular title for the storm god of the Phoenicians.

The question, **"Where is the Prince?"** is even found in Ugaritic literature. It is a form of invocation, to call on the god named to appear and act. In other words, this Tyrian princess was given a name in praise of the chief god of her people (whom the Hebrew Bible refers to mainly by the title **"Baal"**, meaning "lord, master").

"Jezebel" is then a reinterpretation, intended to mock this queen and her god, whom she encouraged Israel to worship.

The name, Jezebel, has come down through the centuries to be used as a general name for all wicked women.

In modern usage, the name of Jezebel is sometimes used as a synonym for sexually promiscuous and sometimes controlling women, as in the title of the 1938 Bette Davis film, "Jezebel", or the 1951 Frankie Lane hit, "Jezebel." This image is epitomized by the phrase "Painted Jezebel." The "painted" part, refers to a line in II Kings just before Jezebel is killed, here she is putting on her makeup.

From a biblical and Christian point of view, a comparison to Jezebel would suggest that a person would be a pagan, or an apostate, **masquerading as a servant of God**, who by manipulation, and/or seduction, misleads the saints of God into sins of idolatry and sexual immorality, making them ineffective. From a Christian point of view, it has also been used to refer to those who challenge evidence and belief in God.

In the New Testament, Jezebel's name is used symbolically as a **false prophetess who seeks to lure Christians into idolatrous practices.** The story of Jezebel is found in 1 Kings chapters 16, 18, 19, 21, and 2 Kings Chapter 9.

REBELLION IS A FORM OF WITCHCRAFT

It's this New Testament ideology that most of us have experienced. Even though the person Jezebel died, this spirit of control is alive and functioning well. This person was influenced by a spirit that controlled the kingdom of Israel through the words and body language of seduction.

I believe that when someone controls another person, there has to be a seducing, smooth, sly, clever spirit present. God never intended for us to control one another. Even as a Senior Leader, I'm not to take advantage of my anointing and power of persuasion to abuse and use people.

The Jezebel spirit is a spirit of control. It is a spirit that desires to rule and run headship for selfish gains. To seduce someone, is to tempt them to do something they normally wouldn't do. This spirit uses the avenue of desire to appeal to those who are weak and haven't yet made up their minds where their loyalties lie.

It's the same thing Satan used in the Garden of Eden in the beginning. Let me inform you, this same spirit and tactic is destroying churches and ministries all over the world.

JEZEBEL DOESN'T WANT TO SIT ON THE THRONE; SHE JUST WANTS TO CONTROL IT

At first glance, these people who enter our ministry appear as someone that is for us and has the headship's best interest at heart. A closer look will reveal they are really about weakening the headship's position and gaining control. The main focus of the spirit of an insurrectionist is to destroy. They are passionate about promoting themselves and they do this by destroying the power, position and influence of the head leader.

The spirit of a Jezebel mainly oppresses, or possesses a woman. You will find this serpent in an environment where the man is weak and the woman is bossy. She will be a person who rules her husband. The man will be submissive and quite in nature. He will be someone who will not speak up and cowards down to her control. In public, they act like they are madly in love, but it's a mask, a front. You can believe that she is calling all the shots in private.

This doesn't mean that all strong women are Jezebels, but it is the atmosphere where this demon will look to enter.

In my opinion, this spirit is the most damaging and dissension creating spirit in the church. This demon has become stronger in the last twenty years, especially since the government of the church has weakened.

What kind of person does the Jezebel look for?

First, it looks for those who are dissatisfied with their life. This spirit looks for someone who is always unhappy and has no joy. It knows that this kind of attitude is easy to persuade and take control of. It feeds on a person who is always complaining about something, someone who dislikes everything, or has something to say negative about most change. Change makes this person nervous.

I had a person on my staff for years that always had a negative attitude. No matter what we did, this person could find the wrong in it... always questioning change; *"why is it needed."* If money was spent the attitude was, *"It cost too much."*

Many times, I would walk in the office before service and others would run in and tell me, "Watch out Bishop, so and so is in one of their moods." I believe when someone is causing people around your office to run from them, they are the breeding ground for a spirit of disloyalty and contention to destroy your ministry.

Be very careful on how you promote joyless people. Joylessness is an inward problem. Those who have discovered who they are in Christ have a powerful inner security. That security will manifest itself in inner joy and peace. This inner stillness and peace will keep them when things aren't always going the right way

Second, those who have a spirit of jealousy... I once had a person on my staff that always asked questions about the money and had a problem spending money for anything. They would call me up when I was not in the office and ask... "Where are you? Why haven't you come in yet?" Anger would shoot up in me. It was not their place to be my boss, especially when I was the one who hired and paid them... I was the person who signed their check. Did they care? No, they didn't respect my office, or my position as a man of God.

I should have fired them the moment I realized they were **un-trainable** and **un-teachable**. Get this! This is very important for unmasking and discerning those who will become disloyal in the end. They may try to defend themselves by convincing you they are just set in their ways. This is a lie! We are *all* able to change through Christ Jesus...

OLD THINGS PASS AWAY...

*"Now we look inside, and what we see is that anyone united with the Messiah gets **a fresh start**, and is **created new**. The old life is gone; a new life begins! Look at it! All this comes from the God who settled the relationship between us and him, and then called us to settle our relationships with each other." 2 Corinthians 5:17-18 Message Bible*

Look also at this translation:

"Therefore, if anyone is in Christ, he is a new creation; old things have passed away; behold, all things have become new. Now all things are of God, who has reconciled us to Himself through Jesus Christ, and has given us the ministry of reconciliation." 2 Corinthians 5:17-19 NKJV

Third, those who have a hidden agenda... These people serve with one objective in their mind; to gain for themselves. These are Jezebel's faithful servants. The whole scheme of Jezebel was Baal worship – which is self worship.

WHAT IS BAAL WORSHIP?

If you walked into any church and asked the audience, **"What is Baal worship?"** you probably wouldn't find too many believers who know. To be sure, most Bible students know that the god, **Baal,** is mentioned over and over again in the Bible. Since most people really don't know what Baal worship is let me give you a little history. Let me begin with a short passage of scripture about the Prophet Elijah.

*"And it came to pass, when Ahab saw Elijah, that Ahab said unto him, Art thou he that troubleth Israel? And he answered, I have not troubled Israel; but thou, and thy father's house, **in that ye have forsaken the commandments of the LORD, and thou hast followed Baalim.**" 1 Kings 18: 17-18 KJV*

Baal worship is the second major religion in the Old Testament. God was really incensed at the possibilities of His people committing to and worshipping this god called Baal. Many believe it is just a religion that faded out in history; don't be mistaken, Baal was not some ancient god. Our society is guilty of modern day Baal worship.

The word, '**Baalim**' is the Hebrew plural for **BAAL, the pagan god of nature and fertility**. I will quote from the Westminster Dictionary of the Bible article on the subject of '**BAAL**' (emphasis mine).

"... Baal worship apparently had its origin in the belief that every tract of ground owed its productivity to a supernatural being, or Baal, that dwelt there. The farmers probably thought that from Baalim, or fertility gods, of various regions, came the increase of crops, fruit and cattle ... The worship of **Baal** was accompanied with lascivious rites (1 Kings 14:24), the sacrifice of children in the fire by parents (Jeremiah 19:5), and kissing the image (1 Kings 19:18; Hosea 13:2). **Baal** was often associated with the goddess, **Astoreth** (Judges 2:13), and in the vicinity of his altar there was often an **Asherah**. (Judges 6:30; 1 Kings 16:32-33, R.V.)"

I know this book isn't about sexuality; however, I want to build a case for this spirit of seduction...

The Westminister dictionary says of the goddess **ASTORETH**:

"... She was the goddess of sexual love, maternity and fertility. Prostitution, as a religious rite, in the service of this goddess under various names is widely attested. The identification of 'Ashtaroth with Aphrodite is evidence of her sexual character."

"Ashtaroth" (plural of Astoreth). In connection with the plural of Baal, a general designation for the female divinities of the Canaanites ... "Asherah", refers to a wooden pole, or mast, which stood at Canaanite places of worship (Exodus 34:13). Originally, it was, perhaps, the trunk of a tree with branches chopped off, and was regarded as the wooden symbol of the goddess Asherah, who, like Ashtoreth, was a type of fertility ... It was erected beside the altar of Baal. (Judges 6:25, 28)"

We can see from these quotes that **Baal** and **Ashtaroth** incorporated illegal sexual acts in their worship and that Asherah was nothing but a phallic symbol. The word 'lascivious' means; lewd, lustful, licentious, lecherous, bawdy. In other words, **Baal worship was accompanied with sinful sexual acts; behavior expressly forbidden in Jehovah's law**. Can you see how this god, called Baal, works through the spirit of seduction? Let us now find out what those forbidden sexual acts were.

We live in a sex crazed world. Sex is the most talked about, sung about, and written about subject in the world. The news and advertising media, not to mention the entertainment world, are all obsessed with sex. **Sex is big business!** Few will doubt this assessment. But what does the **Most High** think about modern man's preoccupation with sex? What does His law say concerning sexual matters? Has He given mankind any instructions as to how we should discipline our sex lives? For the benefit of all who preach the **Elijah Message,** let me quote the Bible on the rights and wrongs of sexual behavior.

The following is **Jehovah's law**: and preachers in today's society will certainly need courage to proclaim it.

Adultery: *"Thou shalt not commit adultery."* Exodus 20: 14 - Sexual acts with a person other than your spouse (Leviticus 20:10, Proverbs 6:32, Jeremiah 23:14).

Fornication/Whoredom: *"Do not prostitute thy daughter, to cause her to be a whore; lest the land fall to whoredom, and the land become full of wickedness."* Leviticus 19: 29

*"Flee fornication. Every sin that a man doeth is without the body; but he that committeth fornication sinneth against his own body."*1 Corinthians 6: *18* - Sexual acts between unmarried persons for pleasure, or profit.

Homosexuality: *"If a man also lie with mankind, as he lieth with a woman, both of them have committed an abomination: they shall surely be put to death; their blood shall be upon them."* Leviticus 20: *13*

"But the men of Sodom were wicked and sinners before the LORD exceedingly." Genesis 13:13

"And the LORD said, Because the cry of Sodom and Gomorrah is great, and because\their sin is very grievous; I will go down now, and see whether they have done altogether according to the cry of it, which is come unto me; and if not, I will know." Genesis 18:20:21

The Apostle Paul wrote about popular sins in his letter to the Romans; particularly the sin of **homosexuality**. Paul said homosexuality is a direct result of rejecting the evidence of creation and refusing to believe in the Creator. (Romans 1:18)

WORD OF IMPORTANCE

This is not my opinion, this is what the Bible declares that Christians are to believe and stand behind. It must be understood, we cannot water down principles because of the fear of persecution. Pastors need to stand up and state the biblical truth. Let's move on and finish this chapter, there is so much I have to say about this subject.

I do understand that this chapter is a little hard to read... It was a little hard to write as well. It took a lot of homework and reading to provide you with this brief synopsis of what is taking place in our churches.

THE DAYS OF NOAH!

In Noah's day, people were preoccupied with **food, drink** and **sex**. Restraint was removed and appetite became a god. Noah preached a warning message for 120 years but to no avail. The population thought the old man was crazy; that he had no idea of what he was talking about. It is exactly the same today. People are obsessed with **food, drink** and **sex**. Another disturbing factor is that it may soon be against the law to condemn the sexual behavior of others. Does this mean that we, who preach the **Elijah Message,** should be silent? I think not. Our commission is to warn mankind of coming judgment, and the matter of sexual sin is in the forefront of our message.

Jesus warned us in the New Testament
"But as the days of Noah were, so shall also the coming of the Son of man be. For as in the days that were before the flood they were eating and drinking, marrying and giving in marriage, until the day that Noah entered into the ark, And knew not until the flood came, and took them all away; so shall also the coming of the Son of man be." Matthew 24:37

"And as it was in the days of Noah, so shall it be also in the days of the Son of man. They did eat, they drank, they married wives, and they were given in marriage, until the day that Noah entered into the ark, and the flood came, and destroyed them all." Luke 17:26

There is, of course, nothing wrong with **eating, drinking** and **getting married;** the human race would cease to exist without these things. The Master was warning that in the last days, just prior to His return, mankind would *give itself over, and* **become obsessed with gluttony, drunkenness and sinful, sexual behavior.** When I use the word **'sinful'** I mean behavior which violates **Divine Law.**

In the Days of Lot

A similar situation developed in the days when the patriarch, **Lot,** lived in **Sodom**; a town which gave its name to the homosexual act between males.

"Likewise also as it was in the days of Lot; they did eat, they drank, they bought, they sold, they planted, and they built; But the same day that Lot went out of Sodom it rained fire and brimstone from heaven, and destroyed them all. Even thus shall it be in the day when the Son of man is revealed." Luke 17: 28

Summary

- **Baal worship** is not just a historical phenomenon. It is widespread, and alive and well in these last days. **Baal worship is giving free reign to the carnal nature.** It expresses itself in gluttony, drunkenness and sinful sexual acts.
- The **Elijah Message** calls people back to the obedience of the commandments of **Yahweh,** the Almighty God of Israel. On the physical level, it denounces sexual sin. On the spiritual level, it denounces the observance of pagan festivals.
- Though the vast majority of mankind will continue to worship **Baal**, there will be many 'overcomers,' believers, who keep the commandments of God and have the faith of **Yeshua, the Messiah (Jesus Christ).** Endeavour to be among that remnant.

To break it down in one phrase, Baal worship is connected to **self-worship**. When you place your desires, your wants and your life above those things God desires for you to have, you have began the life of a Baal worshipper. You are in the position to be seduced and beguiled by the serpent.

THE BEGINNING OF WRONG VOICES

"Now the serpent was more cunning than any beast of the field which the Lord God had made. And he said to the woman, "Has God indeed said, 'You shall not eat of every tree of the garden?" And the woman said to the serpent, "We may eat the fruit of the trees of the garden; but of the fruit of the tree which is in the midst of the garden, God has said, 'You shall not eat it, nor shall you touch it, lest you die.'" Then the serpent said to the woman, "You will not surely die. For God knows that in the day you eat of it your eyes will be opened, and you will be like God, knowing good and evil." So when the woman saw that the tree was good for food, that it was pleasant to the eyes, and a tree desirable to make one wise, she took of its fruit and ate. She also gave to her husband with her, and he ate. Then the eyes of both of them were opened, and they knew that they were naked; and they sewed fig leaves together and made themselves coverings. And they heard the sound of the Lord God walking in the garden in the cool of the day, and Adam and his wife hid themselves from the presence of the Lord God among the trees of the garden. Then the Lord God called to Adam and said to him, "Where are you?" So he said, "I heard Your voice in the garden, and I was afraid because I was naked; and I hid myself." And He said, "Who told you that you were naked? Have you eaten from the tree of which I commanded you that you should not eat?" Then the man said, "The woman whom You gave to be with me, she gave me of the tree, and I ate." And the Lord God said to the woman, "What is this you have done?" The woman said, "The serpent deceived me, and I ate..." Genesis 3:1-14 NKJV

To discover the truth of anything, you must first reach back into its origin and find out how it all started. If we look all the way back into the book of Genesis, Genesis meaning 'beginning,' we will discover how and when this spirit first entered the earth to deceive humans.

God's Church in Complete Harmony

First, we must see how God's garden was in complete harmony. There was perfect peace in the land and with God and man. Everyday God would come down and walk in the Garden of Eden with mankind. Now, this doesn't mean that God left the Garden; God is spirit, God never left. It was just the time of day that God revealed himself to man.

For a while, mankind and God walked together in unity. How can this be? Mankind was not focused on himself. Mankind was focused on God and His eternal purpose on the earth. As long as mankind stayed engrossed with what God was doing and who God was, they were blinded to the fact that they were human... that they were weak... that they weren't eternal. Only God was eternal, but when one looks at something long enough he will believe what he sees.

I believe that the Garden of Eden was a type of the church, and that as long as there was unity to God's vision and God's plan, there was complete communication with God. Mankind was able to walk and talk with God freely.

Somewhere in God's perfect world, everything became confused and disorderly. A place of peace and security became a place where fear, worry and deceit lived.

SATAN IS ALWAYS ATTRACTED TO THOSE WHO ARE MOST LIKE HIM

The serpent was most like the character and nature of Lucifer. *"Now the serpent was more cunning than any beast of the field which the Lord God had made. And he said to the woman..."* The word *"cunning"* means, clever.

CUNNING: *noun*
1. Marked by, or given to artful subtlety and deceptiveness.
2. Executed with, or exhibiting ingenuity.
3. Delicately pleasing; pretty, or cute

of God. It is time to declare, **"JEZEBEL GO TO HELL!"**

Document Your Thoughts

CHAPTER TWO

FIVE MOST DAMAGING INSURRECTIONISTS

"But there was no one like Ahab who sold himself to do wickedness in the sight of the Lord, because Jezebel his wife stirred him up. And he behaved very abominably in following idols, according to all that the Amorites had done, whom the Lord had cast out before the children of Israel."
1 Kings 21:25-26 NKJV

*T*hat verse brings cold chills down my spine. *There was no one like Ahab who sold himself to do wickedness in the sight of God.* How did Ahab fall so low that this verse could be written about him? The Bible tells us that he had a Jezebel who stirred him up. This is the main purpose of those who are sent by the enemy to sabotage our ministries, our families, our friendships and even attempt to abort our destinies if possible.

The phrase *"stirred him up..."* in the Hebrew is defined *as sooth; perhaps denominative; properly, to prick, (i.e. stimulate; by implication, to seduce). To scrub or trash, i.e. wild growth of weeds or briers as if put on the field.* [ii]
Notice the definition of this word in Hebrew means to **sooth, to prick, to stimulate**. Think of how someone is pricked or stimulated. This happens when they are being seduced. Another word that describes the word seduce is entice, tempt, lure, persuade and to beguile. Although Jezebel's name is the most popular name when we want to describe disloyalty, she is not alone. There are five other disloyal spirits that I have discovered.

Five Insurrectionists

Before I name the five, and give you an overview of what they stand for, allow me to explain their connection to us. I believe these characters had spirits in them that caused them to become divisive. I also believe that they represent **five demonic personalities, and that most of us have had to**

fight these demonic personalities at some point in our life to keep unity around us.

I also believe that if we are honest with ourselves, we would have to admit that at least one of these personalities has been active in our own lives.

You are not an insurrectionist just because you have these thoughts or even possess one of these personalities. It becomes a problem when you decide to operate in them and use them for your own selfish gain. You will turn into a wolf in sheep's clothing when you begin to react to your headship in any way that is against Romans chapter 13 and causes you to become angry, jealous or even disobedient.

Let's take a look at these insurrectionists and discover their personalities and infractions.

1. Lucifer   Revelation 12:9
2. Judas   Matthew 27:5
3. Jezebel   I Kings 21:25
4. Absalom   2 Samuel 18:15
5. Ahithophel   2 Samuel 17:23

1. LUCIFER

"Moreover the word of the Lord came to me, saying, "Son of man, take up a lamentation for the king of Tyre, and say to him, 'Thus says the Lord God:"You were the seal of perfection, Full of wisdom and perfect in beauty. You were in Eden, the garden of God; every precious stone was your covering: The sardius, topaz, and diamond, Beryl, onyx, and jasper, Sapphire, turquoise, and emerald with gold. The workmanship of your timbrels and pipes was prepared for you on the day you were created. "You were the anointed cherub who covers; I established you; You were on the holy mountain of God; You walked back and forth in the midst of fiery stones. You were perfect in your ways from the day you were created, till

iniquity was found in you. "By the abundance of your trading You became filled with violence within." Ezekiel 28:11-16 NKJV

Most scholars believe that this really isn't talking just about the king of Tyre, as much as it is a reference to the god who stands behind him, Baal; who is in reality Lucifer. This small passage reveals his creation and his views of who he is and the process to his demise.

When God created Lucifer, he was one of God's leading Angels. The Bible calls them Archangels... We can only find reference to three Archangels.

- Michael
- Gabriel
- Lucifer

Each of these angels had a certain position in heaven before Lucifer fell and was cast down.

Michael was a warring angel. When we see Michael in scriptures, we see him with a sword and power to fight for the cause and purposes of God. Not to say that all angels can't fight, but Michael was assigned to be the leader over warfare.

*"Then he said to me," Do not fear, Daniel, for from the first day that you set your heart to understand, and to humble yourself before your God, your words were heard; and I have come because of your words. But the prince of the kingdom of Persia withstood me twenty-one days; and behold, **Michael, one of the chief princes,** came to help me, for I had been left alone there with the kings of Persia. Now I have come to make you understand what will happen to your people in the latter days, for the vision refers to many days yet to come." Daniel 10:12-14 NKJV*

Daniel prayed to God, and God answered Daniel's prayer immediately, but it took the angelic forces twenty-one days to break through for Daniel to get his answer from God. Notice that it took Michael to bid this warfare against the prince of Persia. Michael, being a chief prince, or ARCHANGEL!

Michael's assignment is to also stand watch over God's people.

"At that time Michael shall stand up, The great prince **who stands watch over the sons of your people***; And there shall be a time of trouble, Such as never was since there was a nation, Even to that time." Daniel 12:1 NKJV*

When God wanted to send someone to gather the bones of Moses, He assigned this job to Michael, and in this verse you will discover the word, ARCHANGEL...

"Yet Michael the archangel, in contending with the devil, when he disputed about the body of Moses, dared not bring against him a reviling accusation, but said, 'The Lord rebuke you!'" Jude 9-10 NKJV

Every time we see the Archangel, Gabriel, it appears that his assignment was to deliver messages that had been sent from the throne of God. I call him the *messenger* angel...

"...the man Gabriel, whom I had seen in the vision at the beginning, being caused to fly swiftly, reached me about the time of the evening offering. And he informed me, and talked with me." Daniel 9:21-22 NKJV

"And the angel answered and said to him, "I am Gabriel, who stands in the presence of God, and was sent to speak to you and bring you these glad tidings." Luke 1:19-20 NKJV

Then there was the third archangel, who was named Lucifer.

"You were the seal of perfection, Full of wisdom and perfect in beauty." Ezekiel 28:12 NKJV

Here's where the problem exists in him. First of all, we must understand that God does not create or promote evil, but at this time angels possessed free will. The problem with free will at this time was that there was no redemptive plan to redeem the angelic host from their decision to disobey.

The problem with Lucifer was that he thought he was perfect. *"Your heart was lifted up because of your beauty; you corrupted your wisdom for the sake of your splendor..." (Ezekiel 28:17 NKJV)* There were no flaws found in him. When God finished His creation... God had made him to be like all the fine and precious jewels on the earth. Thus, he is compared to them in Ezekiel.

"Anything unflawed is an illusion..."

This is why God made man flawed... *"Anything unflawed is an illusion..."* It's our flaws and our weaknesses that drive us to seek out God... His perfections are our goal. We long to walk in His presence because His presence is the only place our weaknesses die. Lucifer was an illusion. He was an illusion to those around him and to himself.

God created Lucifer with the ability to bring Heaven to worship God. He was Heaven's choir director... Heaven's praise and worship band. He had within himself the ability to sing in harmony.

Think about this for a moment... If one can do what they perceive is what God can do; then they may begin to think they are equal to God. The Godhead is made up of three in one; The Father, Son and the Holy Spirit. One divided into three. Satan could be one and, in music, divide himself into three. This gave him the mind-set that he was God's equal. Then he brought all of Heaven to its knees to worship God. When it was time for Lucifer to give God his worship, he would keep some for himself. This caused Lucifer to believe deception. He began to believe his own fan mail... *So he started talking about his perfection.* Lucifer was unable to see his flaws in comparison to God.

The first insurrectionist is a personality that cannot see their own weaknesses and flaws. They believe themselves to be better than those who have been placed over them to lead.

Those in our leadership, or in our church, who are going to fall into this kind of personality, are those who have been given extremely awesome and talented gifts. They can usually be found in the arts department. Their creative side causes them to feel more important. A mind-set begins to develop that they are needed more than anyone else. They begin to develop the attitude of, "You can't do this without me." The truth is that we can. God anoints a plan not a man. God is the Source and Creator of our increase and success...not man! Nor is man's talents and ability the reason why we do what we do. I would rather do it alone than to allow this insurrectionist to stay connected. The truth is that Lucifer *was* flawed. Anyone, or anything, that compares itself to God will always be found wanting.

God intentionally left Himself out of everything He made. We will always end up hollow and empty no matter what we attach ourselves to. This emptiness causes us to seek for something better... something deeper...something, or Someone, with more substance, more love, more joy. That Someone is Jesus! God is the only real source of joy and peace.

His presence is the only place our weakness dies.

2. JUDAS

Judas is the least divisive of the five in my opinion. Judas really loved Jesus. He wanted Jesus to be King. He was willing to sit under His teachings. Judas was for Jesus deep down inside. Those in our leadership, who have a Judas spirit, or personality, can relate. Judas is the person who loves us... who wants to see us rule and have dominion.

Judas' problem was that he wanted to succeed his way instead of God's way. Judas wanted Jesus to set up His Kingdom, but he wanted to win the war by fighting the enemy, not dying for them. Jesus was going to win... He was going to establish a Kingdom that would far outweigh any kingdom that had ever reigned before. This Kingdom would rule the spiritual world first, but Judas didn't want it to happen that way. He wanted Jesus to fight them, not die for them.

> **"Give Judas a rope and he will hang himself..."**

Judas was grief stricken when he saw that he couldn't force Jesus out of His assignment. He couldn't believe it. Jesus was going to die anyway. Judas became depressed and wanted to return the silver that he had taken to betray Jesus.

Judas is the least of my worries when it comes to the five insurrectionists. You don't even have to fight Judas; just give him a rope and he will eventually hang himself.

Watch out for those who want you to succeed their way. They will be the ones who will support you... pay for things...but in the end, they will want you to do it their way. When you refuse, they will betray and leave you.

3. JEZBEL

"But there was no one like Ahab who sold himself to do wickedness in the sight of the Lord, because Jezebel his wife stirred him up." I Kings 21:25

This verse causes chills to run down my back. There was no one like Ahab, who sold himself to do wickedness... because he had a controlling spirit around him that persuaded him to do evil and wrong.

The spirit that is revealed in this insurrectionist is the spirit of control and seduction. In some sense, all of these insurrectionists possess a nature to seduce, or manipulate, but Jezebel is at the top of her game when it comes to control, seduction and manipulation. This spirit's whole demeanor is to control through seduction. To woo you into a decision that you think you made on your own, but in reality you were manipulated and seduced into that decision. This spirit is a master at making you feel in control, but it is behind the scenes doing all the controlling.

This spirit doesn't desire to sit on the throne, stand in the pulpit or lead from the front. No, it wants to hide in the shadows and run the throne, or pulpit, from behind the one anointed to lead. The Jezebel spirit is smooth... It's the same personality that possessed the serpent in the Garden of Eden (Genesis 3:1). The serpent was rallying for control. How did he accomplish that task? By asking Eve questions to gain mastery over what she didn't know. He used subtle language and underlying messages to make it look like Eve was making all the decisions. In the end, it was the spirit in the serpent that was in control. I know you've read it before, but get this in your spirit...

"Whoever has your ear has control over your future..."

When you give your ear to someone, you are no longer deciding your focus and decisions. Those around you, speaking to you, may not be sent to speak to you from God. They may be sent by the enemy to destroy your connection to your destiny. Watch out for those who like to talk to you about what's wrong all the time. These kinds of people may be influenced by the Jezebel spirit.

TIME TO BE EXPOSED

One of the greatest illegitimate and evil powers in the church is an unsanctioned person who calls themselves a prophet, or prophetess; they possess the spirit of control, the spirit of a Jezebel. **I'm not advocating that there is no need for the prophetic word in the last days.** I do understand that there has to be a prophetic word released for any of us to take our next season. However, there are too many in the church who call themselves the voice of God speaking in the office of a prophet, but in reality are just walking in the **spirit of control**...

For years, I sat silently on the sidelines of ministry hoping that God would expose such people in my church... I would sit and watch as this spirit wouldn't leave. As a matter of fact, one of the reasons it takes so long to discover this spirit is because it appears to be the one who is in support of what you're doing. Especially to your face, but behind your back watch out... they are building a following. Those who carry a spirit of insurrection will always try to build a following to their way of thinking. I don't care how much I prayed, fasted and cried to the Lord about the Jezebel, it just wouldn't leave.

Here's a fact! They will never leave until you stand up and confront them. The longer you hesitate the greater the risk of destroying the innocent in your leadership and church. When you wait you allow the poison of their ***toxic venom, which is their voice, to spread into the ears of many.*** At this point you may lose others when you remove them. This saddens me because the innocent suffer for the disobedient act of the guilty.

SIGNS THAT PROMOTE THE ATMOSPHERE FOR A JEZEBEL SPIRIT TO EXIST

1. *An overly powerful woman married to a weak willed husband... He never stands his ground or raises the standard in his own house.*
2. *Someone who is always trying to gain access to the headship... They ignore protocol.*
3. *A person who loves to use words of flattery too much. They do this to gain access, ego scratchers can be deadly. Remember, the same crowd that yelled, "Crucify*

Him," in the end was the same crowd that praised Jesus in the beginning.
4. *Sexual and sensual in their actions.*
5. *They're overly flirty. These people have an agenda.*
6. *Will agree to your face, but always question your decisions behind the leader's back.*
7. *Someone with marital issues and problems.*
8. *A woman who likes to show off her features be noticed.*

Caution: These are signs only! They are not always revealing a Jezebel Spirit- just the door it can enter into the atmosphere. A Jezebel spirit is mostly a spirit that controls through women; however at times it can use a man.

4. ABSALOM

"After this it happened that Absalom provided himself with chariots and horses, and fifty men to run before him. Now Absalom would rise early and stand beside the way to the gate. So it was, whenever anyone who had a lawsuit came to the king for a decision, that Absalom would call to him and say, "What city are you from?" And he would say, "Your servant is from such and such a tribe of Israel." Then Absalom would say to him, "Look, your case is good and right; but there is no deputy of the king to hear you." Moreover Absalom would say, "Oh that I were made judge in the land, and everyone who has any suit or cause would come to me; then I would give him justice." And so it was, when-ever anyone came near to bow down to him that he would put out his hand and take him and kiss him. In this manner Absalom acted toward all Israel who came to the king for judgment. So Absalom stole the hearts of the men of Israel." 2 Samuel 15:1-6 NKJV

The fourth insurrectionist is the spirit of Absalom. Absalom was one of King David's sons. He was noted for his personal beauty and for the extraordinary abundance of the hair on his head (2 Samuel 14:25, 26).

Absalom represents the people in our ministries who are **UNGRATEFUL**. They possess the "all about me" attitude. The wound of rejection is over magnified in their attitude by the way others see and treat them. Absalom was a very good-looking man. However, he did not see himself as someone who had a secure identity. He used his external ways to make himself feel better internally. The ungrateful will always be those who are offended easily. They will be the people who want to sit at the entrance of the house listening to complaints about the leader. They may not talk, but they will surely give an ear. Let's look at how this spirit is born in our ministries.

> "Never give mercy where God has declared judgment..."

The first public act of Absalom's life was the bloody revenge he executed against Amnon, David's eldest son, who had basely wronged Absalom's sister, Tamar. This revenge was executed at the time of the festivities connected with a great sheep-shearing at Baal-hazor.

David's other sons fled from the place in horror, and brought the tidings of the death of Amnon to Jerusalem. Alarmed for the consequences of the act, Absalom fled to his grandfather at Geshur, and there lived for three years (2 Samuel 3:3; 13:23-38). Here's where King David made a grave mistake.

David overlooked one of God's commandments. His love for his son, Absalom blinded him from what God had commanded in the law; "An eye for and eye and a tooth for a tooth." David, by God's law, was supposed to kill Absalom for taking revenge and killing Amnon. Instead of doing what was required of a king, and not just a father, David brought trouble and division into his kingdom. So instead of killing Absalom, David exiled him from the kingdom... he wasn't allowed at the king's court. David mourned his absent son, now branded with the guilt of fratricide. David decided to invite Absalom back to Jerusalem, but two years elapsed before his father admitted him into his presence (2 Samuel 14:28). Absalom was now probably the oldest surviving son of David, and as he was of royal descent by his mother, as well as by his father, he began to aspire to the throne. His pretensions were favored by the people. By many means, he gained their affection; and after his return from Geshur (2 Samuel 15:7; margin notes, Revised Version) he went up to Hebron, the old capital of Judah, along with a great body of the people, and there proclaimed himself to be king.

THOUGHT: *Watch out for those who want to sit in the back and talk to everyone about the church and the ministry except the leader. Those who are unthankful for the mercy of the Senior Pastor may want to take his church, or ministry...*

The revolt was so successful that David found it necessary to leave Jerusalem and flee to Mahanaim, beyond Jordan; where upon Absalom returned to Jerusalem and took possession of the throne without opposition.

THOUGHT: *When you don't do what God's commanded, expect to lose your position and throne. David wouldn't fight him because he knew he was wrong in not carrying out God's laws.*

"You Can't Complain About What You Tolerate."

The Absalom spirit rests on those who may not always do the talking, but they will most assuredly do the listening. They become garbage cans for the grief of others. Verse 2 says that Absalom would sit at the gate to hear the complaints of the people. Gates, in the Bible, always refer to access. When Jacob laid his head on a stone and fell asleep, he dreamed of angels ascending and descending... he said I found the gate of Heaven. He was actually saying I found Heaven's access.

When the man in Acts chapter three was laid at the gate called Beautiful, he was sitting at the place of access. This man was about to meet the man he was destined to be. It's at this access gate where change will take place.

Absalom sat at the access of where he could get into the hearts of the people. Why? So he could turn their hearts away from the king, the leader. There are many who sit in our churches... They sit in the rear, or the back of the church, they stand at the entrance with one thing in mind, to hear the complaints of the people. The Absalom spirit is usually a person who has been wounded and rejected because of something they did. Instead of healing and allowing time to create access back into the presence of the leader, they sit in the outskirts bidding and listening to gain the acceptance of those around them, so they can feel approved and accepted in their pain of rejection.

This spirit sympathizes with those who are wounded instead of standing up and helping them not lose their way, or their connection to the king... ***"Then Absalom would say to him, "Look, your case is good and right; but there is no deputy of the king to hear you."*** *(2 Samuel 15:3)* This causes the person who is wounded to gain acceptance from the people. Let me caution you, it's not the people you want to stay in covenant with, it's the KING... to do that, you are going to have to stay connected to those God has placed over you, whether you like them or not.

"So Absalom stole the hearts of the men of Israel." 2 Samuel 15:6

This spirit is about stealing the hearts of the people. Heart means *mind*. The Absalom spirit is a 'mind stealer.' The mind decides your focus. Whatever the mind focuses on, the will begins to believe.

- ***Your mind bosses your emotions...***
- ***Your emotions decide your feelings...***

- *Your feelings usually decide what you connect to...*

These people had no chance. They were deceived into believing that Absalom was their king.

The Absalom spirit are those who leave the ordained headship of the senior pastor and go, unsanctioned by God, to start their own work, their own church; sitting in their living room because they can't sit under and submit to the Set Man!

CHARACTER OF THE ABSALOM SPIRIT

1. A Phony Compassion... Don't be deceived by how this spirit acts in its compassion. Absalom's compassion is solely connected to his own selfish mind. He knows that the attitude of the people can decide his wealth and position. His compassion is directly connected to his ambition and not his heart for the people. These kinds of people are all over our churches. They try to appear interested in others for the sake of the people they are helping, but in the end, they are working for their own agenda. Absalom worked through gossip and flattery. Remember, gossip is saying something about someone behind their back that you wouldn't say to their face. Flattery is saying something to someone's face that you wouldn't say behind their back.

2. A Stealthy Connection... Be very cautious of people who want to meet in secret. They always want to talk to you on the phone or away from the leadership. These people are attempting to connect you to their rebellion. Sometimes they will do it without you even noticing it. They can create so much confusion that you become offended with the headship when you weren't really mad at them at all. You were manipulated to find an offense. The sad thing is that you are guilty in the eyes of the Lord for treason; for being a disloyal member. Let me warn you now. This spirit will throw you under the bus when it is finished with you. It has no problem sacrificing you for its gain.

Guard your heart and don't become discontent. Discontented people will always try to enlist others. They will always want someone to be in agreement to their pain.

Watch out for the spirit of rebellion. Rebellious people will always create division to benefit their cause. They will create a mind of vengeance to destroy what usually has corrected them. Rebellion is the byproduct of someone who doesn't want to be corrected. Correction will usually flesh out and expose rebellion.

3. A Cunning Contention... Cunning means *clever; impure mandate.* People with the Absalom spirit will always try to take matters into their own hands instead of approaching the headship to get instructions. They believe they are above the law, the church or organization's government and rules.

They will lift themselves up and proclaim to be above correction. They appear to be better and know more than those who are leading. Absalom spirit believes the end justifies the means. In the end, it reveals they have no fear of God.

BREEDING GROUND FOR THE ABSALOM SPIRIT TO GROW (2 Samuel Chapters 13 – 15)

1. Offense, hatred, un-forgiveness and bitterness.
2. A basic distrust and resentment of one's authority either justifiable, or exaggerated.
3. A basic independence and self-dependence-especially as it pertains to honest communication, problem solving, sharing of honest feelings, needs, wants, etc.
4. An Absalom Spirit is rooted in camouflaged bitterness-unresolved disappointments, fear, anger, impotence, etc.
5. An Absalom Spirit is rooted in irrational secrets-that appear totally rational and justified to the "Absalom."
6. An Absalom Spirit is rooted in hidden agendas, hidden strategies and hidden alliances. **Key is hidden.**
7. An Absalom Spirit is rooted in hidden contempt, hidden hatred and hidden revenge-of authority and those under

that authority.

8. An Absalom Spirit is rooted in pride.

9. An Absalom Spirit is rooted in rebellion-that will continue to grow and become unquenchable.

10. An Absalom Spirit is rooted in a deep-seated desire to be close to, next to, or in a place of favor with the one in authority, but not with purity of heart.

11. An Absalom Spirit is rooted in impressing and stealing the hearts of the people who are under authority in order to eventually "dethrone" and replace the one in authority.

MANIFESTATIONS OF THE ABSALOM SPIRIT

1. An Absalom Spirit manifests in attitude of self-promotion that is focused on what they get and not who they serve.

2. An Absalom Spirit manifests in a carefully constructed and carefully projected self-image that is designed to impress. Their only focus is what you see them do. In private they do nothing. In public and around the leader they appear to be the one who is doing all the work. They have no problem giving you their stats while throwing others under the bus. Always advancing at the expense of others. They appear to be humble, loyal, caring and busy, but I assure you it is all a ruse.

3. An Absalom Spirit manifests in manipulation. They love to control others. This control is done in the picturesque colors that appear they are helping when they are actually forcing their own issues to come to life.

4. An Absalom Spirit uses the avenue of servant hood, but manifests in selfish ambition that is disguised as service to others.

5. An Absalom Spirit manifests in a spirit of divisiveness,

antagonism, and negative criticism of those in authority to promote self. They sit in your enemy's presence discussing you.

6. An Absalom Spirit manifests in rebellion. No matter what you do or say in the end they rebel.

7. An Absalom Spirit manifests in false humility.

8. An Absalom Spirit manifests in thievery--stealing the hearts and loyalty of the people away from their true authority. They do this by acting like they care more for the people than the leader.

9. An Absalom Spirit manifests in treachery. This spirit sits discusses all your weaknesses. They get to know you so that they can expose you.

10. An Absalom Spirit manifests in subtle seduction.

11. An Absalom Spirit manifests in religious hypocrisy and hype. "...While offering sacrifices..." Their sacrifices are for show...not to support the vision. At first glance they appear to be the most supportive person, but they are dangerous.

12. An Absalom spirit is ungrateful. It didn't matter to Absalom that he was supposed to be judged and punished. David spared Absalom's life, but he was angry because he couldn't be on the throne. Watch out for those who are ungrateful and unthankful.

13. Absalom makes everyone feel like they are not being judged in his presence, but judges everyone in their absence.

LIES THE ABSALOM SPIRIT BELIEVES

1. Most authority is not to be trusted.
2. Most authority is incompetent.
3. The attitude, "I know the right way to handle this."
4. I'm as skilled and as anointed as the head.
5. God speaks to us all; not just to the pastor.

REASONS WHY THIS SPIRIT IS DIFFCULT TO DEAL WITH

1. People are emotionally attached to them through relationships.
2. Absalom is nice, lovable, good looking and popular. Everyone loved Absalom, even King David. The leader is deceived. They give this spirit too much time to connect because they refuse to see their true colors.
3. If the pastor corrects them it appears that they are being non-Christian and unloving. However, the only way to deal with them is to cut them off. David wouldn't have had any problems if he had not let Absalom back into the kingdom.

   Many times those who operate in an Absalom spirit will leave a church out of rebellion, but want to stay connected through fellowship. They will use this reasoning, *"We are still apart of the kingdom of God even if we are not in the same church."*

   Though this logic sounds good, it is not. Looking at their history and the fact that they caused division are indicators their true motive is not for fellowship. Their true motive is to continue to influence and manipulate.

4. If the pastor tries to discuss them to others it makes him and his leadership appear paranoid and fearful.

SIGNS THAT INDICATE YOU HAVE AN ABSALOM IN YOUR LIFE

1. *They seek an audience...* *"Now Absalom would rise early and stand beside the way to the gate. So it was, whenever anyone who had a lawsuit came to the king for a decision, that Absalom would call to him and say, "What city are you from?" And he would say, "Your servant is from such and such a tribe of Israel."* 2 Samuel 15:2

2. *Love, kindness and favor are their tools. Who can resist that?* They are not committed nor can they be corrected. They give favors, or access to build a persuasion against the church, not to build it.

3. *Absalom appears to be concerned and uses a false kindness to steal the hearts of those who are connected to the headship...* Watch out for those who like to befriend someone the pastor is close to. Their focus is to gain access to those who have the pastor's ear. Then they steal their ear to destroy them.

4. *Uses words of flattery such as...* *"You are special to me. I love you more than the pastor; I will spend the quality time with you that he doesn't."*

5. *Gives Special treatment...* Coffee, Tea, fellowship, trips, gifts and favors. Everyone likes to be treated special. Everyone wants to feel special. When this spirit is at work they will remind you in the future of the gifts they gave you. Expose them quickly.

6. *Has an attitude that nothing the pastor or leadership does is good enough. They can always do it better...* Even if most of Absalom's ideas are implemented it will never be good enough. Fault will always be found.

7. *They plant doubt in the minds of the followers concerning leadership...* They find faults in leaders usually not related to spiritual qualifications, and minor

things are made major issues...

8. ***They always have a hidden agenda...*** Absalom's motive was not known until it manifested and it was too late. You know where you stand with Jezebel and Korah, but Absalom is sneaky, and does things behind your back.

9. ***This spirit always tells you what you want to hear, not what you need to hear to change...*** A pastor's job is to speak the truth in love; sometimes that truth hurts and requires change, but it is always for our good.

10. ***They eventually come forward with open rebellion, disloyalty and cause division.***

Move swiftly away from an Absalom when you become aware that you may be involved with or listening to that spirit. **<u>Tell your pastor</u>** immediately. You will fall if you stay connected with him. The only cure from this bite is to expose them.

5. AHITHOPHEL

"For it is not an enemy who reproaches me; Then I could bear it. Nor is it one who hates me who has exalted himself against me; Then I could hide from him. But it was you, a man my equal, My companion and my acquaintance. We took sweet counsel together, And walked to the house of God in the throng. Let death seize them; Let them go down alive into hell, For wickedness is in their dwellings and among them. As for me, I will call upon God, And the Lord shall save me. Evening and morning and at noon I will pray, and cry aloud, And He shall hear my voice. He has redeemed my soul in peace from the battle that was against me, For there were many against me. God will hear, and afflict them, Even He who abides from of old. Because they do not change, Therefore they do not fear God." Psalm 55:12-19 NKJV

Ahithophel and David were the best of friends. In the kingdom, they were like peaches and cream... Roy Rogers and Trigger... Batman and Robin. They were the "dynamic due." They belonged together.

Ahithophel was the king's counselor, he was never wrong when he gave counsel to David. The bible declared that his was the oracle of God. Ahithophel became David's best friend (1 Chronicles 27:33 NKJV).

"Now the advice of Ahithophel, which he gave in those days, was as if one had inquired at the oracle of God. So was all the advice of Ahithophel..." 2 Samuel 16:23 NKJV

Ahithophel made up for what David lacked in political conversation. David was a man of war. David knew how to fight and to strategize in battle, but in times of peace David was a fish out of water. So Ahithophel was David's right hand. One day David woke up and found that His friend and companion had traded sides and was now found in the enemy's camp. Ahithophel became the counselor to Absalom; David couldn't believe it. David's heart was full of pain and anguish, but regardless of how David felt, he would not fight what God had anointed.

In Psalm 55 David writes. *"It's not my enemy who reproaches me... Then, I could bear it! Fight it! God it is not one who hates me who has exalted himself against me; then I would, or could hide from him. But it was you, Ahithophel, a man of my equal, my friend, my acquaintance. We took sweet counsel together; we walked to the house of God together. Oh God! Let death seize me, or them. I can't fight this man, who never missed your counsel."*

David's heart was heavy, but before you start hating Ahithophel let me tell you the rest of the story. What caused this once loyal and close confidant to turn?

It was the season for the kings to go to war. Instead of doing what was required, David decided to do what he felt. So he sent his army. One of the men in that army was Uriah, the Hittite.

Instead of David being with his army, he stayed back and spent a night standing on the roof of his house where he saw a young, beautiful woman bathing. He began to lust for her and had her summoned to his chambers (2 Samuel 11:2). Bathsheba, who was Uriah's wife, lay with David and conceived. David, knowing that this was wrong, began the plot to cover his sins. He sent for Uriah, who was on the battlefield, where David was supposed to be. He then tried to orchestrate a lie and manipulate a scenario where Uriah would lay with Bathsheba. Uriah, being so devoted and loyal to David, wouldn't even consider sleeping in his house, or with his wife. When David realized that things weren't going to happen the way he had planned, He sent word to have Uriah killed in battle.

Here's where the plot thickens. How does Uriah, who is a Hittite, become an officer in the king's army? He married Bathsheba, and Bathsheba was the granddaughter of Ahithophel. Uriah was promoted because of Ahithophel and his connection to David. This is the reason Ahithophel ran from David's leadership.

Imagine the questions that went through the mind of Ahithophel. David could have had any woman he wanted. *"Why did you lay with my granddaughter? David, we were friends. We ate together... We worshipped together... How could you have done this to my family?"*

Now the script has changed. Are you feeling a little angry at David? I did! I became frustrated at how David could have done this to his friend.

Ahithophel left David's camp and entered Absalom's camp. Even God was angry with David. In Absalom's camp, Ahithophel began to lay out the plans to capture David.

Get a mental picture of this. David was laying on the floor in the King's chamber, crying to God about Ahithophel saying, *"God if he comes, I will not fight him. I will not touch what you've anointed."* On the other side of the coin,

Ahithophel was talking to Absalom about what to do to David and how it should be done.

"And Ahithophel said to Absalom, "Go in to your father's concubines, whom he has left to keep the house; and all Israel will hear that you are abhorred by your father. Then the hands of all who are with you will be strong." So they pitched a tent for Absalom on the top of the house, and Absalom went in to his father's concubines in the sight of all Israel. Now the advice of Ahithophel, which he gave in those days, was as if one had inquired at the oracle of God. So was all the advice of Ahithophel both with David and with Absalom. Moreover Ahithophel said to Absalom, "Now let me choose twelve thousand men, and I will arise and pursue David tonight. **I will come upon him while he is weary and weak, and make him afraid. And all the people who are with him will flee, and I will strike only the king.** *Then I will bring back all the people to you. When all return except the man whom you seek, all the people will be at peace." And the saying pleased Absalom and all the elders of Israel."* 2 Samuel 16:21-17:4 NKJV

Notice Ahithophel says, *"Let me strike only the king. Let me kill him."* This is where the Lord changed his mind about the judgment of David. David was wrong for what he had done was going to be judged... but by God not those under his leadership.

Ahithophel, even though he had a cause to be mad, hurt and even angry, had no right to raise his hand against what God had anointed. This is the problem with the attitude of the spirit of Ahithophel.

The church has taken hold of the idea that we have a right to attack those God has placed over us and anointed to lead us because of their exposed flaws and weaknesses; however, according to God's standards, we have no right to attack at all.

In the twenty-first century church, we attack and do harm when we talk about God's leaders. Our conversation and our words can beat down more leaders than an army of swords.

What happened to Ahithophel?

"Now when Ahithophel saw that his advice was not followed, he saddled a donkey, and arose and went home to his house, to his city. Then he put his household in order, and hanged himself, and died; and he was buried in his father's tomb." 2 Samuel 17:23 NKJV

He hung himself. He knew that God had not given him the authority to touch David. His anger got the best of him. In the end, all of those who rise up against God's anointed pay a tremendous price. They are all dealt with in the end.

"Never touch a Man of God while he is in transition."

If you have listened, talked about or had anger that caused you to rise up in word, or deed, against any man or woman of God, repent right now! Repentance is God's greatest gift. Don't hesitate, do it right now before you end up destroying everything in your house. God is not pleased with you. You have no right to touch God's man or woman no matter how much you believe you are justified.

In the Gospel of John, we read that Mary went to the tomb where Jesus was buried. She noticed that the stone in front of the tomb had been moved and the entrance was open. Jesus was standing beside the entrance, but Mary assumed it was the gardner.

How could this be? How could a woman who had walked with Jesus, forgiven by Him, fed Him and sat under His teachings not recognize Him when He stood before her?

Jesus had stepped into a different dimension. He was not the Jesus who died; He was becoming the Jesus who would sit at the right hand of the Father. She didn't recognize His appearance, but when Jesus said, *"Mary,"* she immediately knew who He was. Why? She recognized His voice. She was connected to His voice, His teaching. As soon as she recognized Jesus' voice she said, *"Master, Teacher,"* and reached out to cling to and touch Him.

Jesus moved back and said, *"Mary don't touch me. I have not yet made full change, or transition. I am not the man I was; however, I am not the man I'm yet supposed to be."* Never touch a man or woman of God while they are in transition. You could hinder the greatest change in their lives and in yours. After Jesus ascended to God, He came back and informed the disciples, and the church, that we have the victory. We now have victory over life, death and the enemy.

I've seen it so many times. The pastor starts acting, walking and talking different. Those who have been with them for a while notice their change. They say things like, *"You're not the same, you act different. You talk different. I liked you better when you were who you use to be."* These people are fools. No one will ever change or be different if the leader stays the same. I'm going to say it again, **do not touch a man or woman of God during change.** Allow them to change. Stay connected even though you feel uncomfortable. I promise you will not be disappointed when you enter your next season with them.

WHERE HAS THE POWER GONE?

My spirit is heavy as I look around and see what has become of the local church. The average church attendee doesn't last more than five years; this really concerns me. There was a time in the local church that people were committed no matter what. Now, it doesn't take much for people to uproot people and continue on an endless journey to hunt out the church that stimulates them. What we need in the church is not stimulation but cultivation.

You would think that Christians would more powerful; that they would be full of freedom and love for people. However, it seems that we are more angry and full of bitterness. Anger and un-forgiveness, and other such issues can become doors that allow the words of the insurrectionist to find root and cause people to become disloyalty.

Jesus told us to do good, seek justice, rebuke the oppressor, defend the fatherless, plead for the widow, heal the sick and cast out demons as God has instructed. *(Isaiah 1:17-Mark 16:17-18).*

Instead, it seems that we find most churches, and their people *anemic, spiritually impotent* and in *bondage.* Of course, I'm not speaking about all churches, but most seem to be a place where the organization is more powerful than the organism. Many churches have embraced the mind-set that they are holding the fort till Jesus comes instead of taking the land; however, in reality they are not holding anything. They are full of hurting and unchanged people who are not living victorious lives, but living in the pains of their past. We all have a past. We all have some sort of hurting wound from the season of yesterday.

We must learn how to use the past for our advantage. Learn from it, not live in it; embrace where we've come from. We were given power to tread upon the enemies head

"Anything Uncontested Will Flourish."

(Luke 10). Jesus gave the church power over unclean spirits, to cast them out, and to heal all kinds of sickness and disease. We are supposed to walk free from controlling spirits. Many who call themselves Christians may not be disciples of Jesus because they don't have any power except to *criticize, backbite, fight, complain, rebel, doubt and pout*! However, whatever is born of God overcomes the world, and this is the victory that has overcome the world-***our faith***. When we accept Jesus Christ as our Savior, Lord and King, the victory now resides in us by the faith God gave us. God is able to do exceedingly abundantly above all that we ask or think (Ephesians 3:20).

A lot of the problems in our churches are due to the leadership walking in toleration of issues instead of confronting them. Anything uncontested flourishes.

The Bible is clear on how we should deal with these spirits. It is time for the body of Christ to stand up and take authority over the spirit of disloyalty!

CHAPTER THREE

CONFRONTING THE SPIRIT OF DISLOYALTY

BINDING TOGETHER

*T*he first and most deadly weapon to confront and overcome the spirit of disloyalty is exposure. Pastors in the same city need to inform one another of such people who leave their church. This would at least make the next pastor aware of such people. This will help them make sure disloyal people are not making connection to their sheep with a hidden agenda to disconnect them from headship.

If you have been lulled by this kind of person repent and cut off the relationship as fast as you can. If you have sat in such meetings with those who talk, criticize and seem to think they are above the man or woman that God has ordained as your pastor, then run! Run as fast as you can away from these demonic controlled people who have been possessed for the advancement of hell. God will forgive you. Expose them to your leaders immediately.

I am spending a lot of time on this one insurrectionist because it's the meanest and hardest one to expose.

If you're feeling a little weak about what I am saying just pray... I promise you I am being biblically sound. You can't make friends with this spirit or any person being influenced by this spirit. Trust me, most of the time this person is unreachable because they are unwilling to see that they are the problem.

Years ago I had a women's prayer group that met every week. They would come in, sit in the sanctuary and supposedly pray for me, my family and the vision of the church. They met for years, but something in me didn't feel right about it.

I began to notice how these women treated their husbands... too authoritative and resistant to correction. Something in me started to worry about what was really going on in my intercessory prayer group. I decided to go in and sit in the back of the sanctuary just to observe them. I found out they did very little praying for me. These women would sit around a table in the room and talk about what God was saying to them about the church, the staff and the ministry. One particular person was always leading the group. She would orchestrate and lead the conversation. I sat in amazement at how long they talked before they began to pray. Then, their prayer would get all crazy and loud; super spiritual so to speak. They walked around screaming in tongues, praying and prophesying to one another. It was like a coven of women building up their own agenda. My heart was pumping faster than normal; I left in horror. This is when I began to study on the spirit of the Jezebel.

When that prayer session was over I asked the leader if that was a typical intercession session. She said, "Oh yes! God is so faithful to us." The woman that was leading them was an awesome woman. She was a good wife and a great mother, but something in me began to sense something wasn't right.

After I completed my study on this spirit, I decided, as the Senior Pastor, to sit in on their little prayer session. When they started talking about "what God was saying to them," I spoke up and said, *"I don't want us to talk today about what the Lord is saying to each other; however, I do want to talk to you about what the Lord is saying and teaching me."* I began to speak and teach about the **"JEZEBEL SPIRIT;"** the spirit of control. Let me tell you right now, I was freaking out. The more I spoke, the more the spirit of the Lord was falling on what I was saying. Some of those women's countenance became horrifying expressions. I could actually see their faces changing. It looked like demons looking back at me. They became agitated and restless. When I announced I was going to do a whole series on this subject they became angry.

After the meeting, one woman came up to me crying. She said, *"Please don't teach on that subject."*

I said, *"Why?"*

She said, *"Because, every time a preacher talks about that, I have to leave the church."* WOW! Can you believe that? That day I shut down their little gathering. I found out that this was one of the places the enemy was using to gain control in my ministry, and it took years for me and my church to overcome its affects.

"Beware of false prophets, who come to you in sheep's clothing, but inwardly they are ravenous wolves. You will know them by their fruits. Do men gather grapes from thorn bushes or figs from thistles? Even so, every good tree bears good fruit, but a bad tree bears bad fruit. A good tree cannot bear bad fruit, nor can a bad tree bear good fruit. Every tree that does not bear good fruit is cut down and thrown into the fire. Therefore by their fruits you will know them." Matthew 7:15-20 NKJV

"And have no fellowship with the unfruitful works of darkness, but rather expose them. For it is shameful even to speak of those things, which are done by them in secret, But all things that are exposed are made manifest by the light, for whatever makes manifest is light..." Ephesians 5:11-14 NKJV

That one incident nearly cost me everything.

I have been through so much because one of my greatest weaknesses is walking with wrong people too long. My need to fix people has placed me in bad situations. When I should have let them go, I stayed connected, and it cost me dearly in the end.

THE MAN OF GOD ALONE DOESN'T POSSESS THE POWER TO CONQUER THIS DEMON!

It is going to take a team effort to win the battle of control from the pew in our churches. Those in the pew have to be in covenant and connect to those in the pulpit. Again, this is not to say that we are to allow those in the pulpit to live sinful lives. It is to say, that loyalty to the pulpit will not go unrewarded by God, and that God will punish disloyalty in the end.

UNDERSTANDING WHO GOD CHOOSES TO SPEAK THROUGH

When God speaks what does He sound like, or whom will He sound like? God usually only speaks through those He has placed over us. When God speaks to us as individuals, He will have those over us confirm that those were His words. This is not taught in most churches, especially the United States.

We do not want a church led by someone; we want a church led by democracy. However, when we read the word of God, we discover the Lord spoke to the headship, not the congregation, when we wanted to speak or give instructions. Look at these chapter headings in the book of Numbers.

- Numbers chapter one... **"Now the Lord spoke to Moses..."**
- Numbers chapter two... **"And the Lord spoke to Moses and Aaron..."**
- Numbers chapter three... **"The Lord spoke with Moses..."**
- Numbers chapter four.... **"Then the Lord spoke to Moses and Aaron saying..."**
- Numbers chapter five... **"And the Lord spoke to Moses, saying...."**
- Numbers chapter six... **"Then the Lord spoke to Moses saying..."**
- Numbers chapter seven... **"Then the Lord spoke to Moses, saying..."**
- Numbers chapter eight... **"And the Lord spoke to Moses, saying..."**
- Numbers chapter nine... **"Now the Lord spoke to Moses in the wilderness of Sinai..."**
- Numbers chapter ten... **"And the Lord spoke to Moses, saying..."**

Notice what happened as soon as the pattern changed and the people tried to involve themselves in the process of how God works His government.

*"Now when the people complained, **it displeased the Lord; for the Lord heard it, and His anger was aroused. So the fire of the Lord burned among them, and consumed some in the outskirts of the camp.**" Numbers 11:1-2 NKJV*

In Numbers chapter 12, Miriam and Aaron spoke against Moses and the Lord came down to punish them...

"Then Miriam and Aaron spoke against Moses because of the Ethiopian woman whom he had married; for he had married an Ethiopian woman. So they said, "Has the Lord indeed spoken only through Moses? Has He not spoken through us also?" And the Lord heard it." Numbers 12:1-2

"Suddenly the Lord said to Moses, Aaron, and Miriam, "Come out, you three, to the tabernacle of meeting!" So the three came out. Then the Lord came down in the pillar of cloud and stood in the door of the tabernacle, and called Aaron and Miriam. And they both went forward. Then He said, 'Hear now My words: If there is a prophet among you, I, the Lord, make Myself known to him in a vision; I speak to him in a dream. Not so with My servant Moses; He is faithful in all My house. I speak with him face to face, Even plainly, and not in dark sayings; And he sees the form of the Lord. Why then were you not afraid to speak against My servant Moses?" So the anger of the Lord was aroused against them, and He departed. And when the cloud departed from above the tabernacle, suddenly Miriam became leprous, as white as snow. Then Aaron turned toward Miriam, and there she was, a leper. So Aaron said to Moses, "Oh, my lord! Please do not lay this sin on us, in which we have done foolishly and in which we have sinned. Please do

not let her be as one dead, whose flesh is half consumed when he comes out of his mother's womb!" So Moses cried out to the Lord, saying, "Please heal her, O God, I pray!" Then the Lord said to Moses, "If her father had but spit in her face, would she not be shamed seven days? Let her be shut out of the camp seven days, and afterward she may be received again." So Miriam was shut out of the camp seven days, and the people did not journey till Miriam was brought in again. And afterward the people moved from Hazeroth and camped in the Wilderness of Paran." Numbers 12:1-13:1 NKJV

Notice at the end it was Moses, the head, who interceded for those who were speaking against headship. This is after God opened the earth and swallowed over twenty thousand.

Numbers chapter 13, *"And God spoke to Moses."* Who does God sound like when He speaks? He sounds like the man or woman of God that you are sitting under.

How does the spirit of Jezebel work? This spirit seduces through words. When you give your ear to her, you have decided your future and may have decided the demise of your church and pastor.

Still not convinced of this one point? Have you ever read the story about a woman in the Bible named Hannah? Being barren, she prayed, fasted and made a covenant with God that if He would do the miraculous and give her a son, she would give him to the temple to be trained for ministry.

God heard her prayers, agreed to her covenant and gave her a child. She named him Samuel. She took Samuel to the temple when he was weaned from her breast to be raised and trained under the leadership of the High Priest, Eli. **"But Samuel ministered before the Lord, even as a child, wearing a linen ephod." 1 Samuel 2:18 NKJV**

"Now the boy Samuel ministered to the Lord before Eli. And the word of the Lord was rare in those days; there was no widespread revelation. And it came to pass at that time, while

*Eli was lying down in his place, and when his eyes had begun to grow so dim that he could not see, and before the lamp of God went out in the tabernacle of the Lord where the ark of God was, and while Samuel was lying down, that the Lord called Samuel. And he answered, "Here I am!" So he ran to Eli and said, "Here I am, for you called me." And he said, "I did not call; lie down again." And he went and lay down. Then the Lord called yet again, "Samuel!" So Samuel arose and went to Eli, and said, "Here I am, for you called me." He answered, "I did not call, my son; lie down again." (**Now Samuel did not yet know the Lord, nor was the word of the Lord yet revealed to him**.) And the Lord called Samuel again the third time. So he arose and went to Eli, and said, "Here I am, for you did call me."* **Then Eli perceived that the Lord had called the boy**. *Therefore Eli said to Samuel, "Go, lie down; and it shall be, if He calls you, that you must say, 'Speak, Lord, for your servant hears.'" So Samuel went and lay down in his place. Now the Lord came and stood and called as at other times, "Samuel! Samuel!" And Samuel answered, "Speak, for your servant hears."* **Then the Lord said to Samuel**.*" 1 Samuel 3:1-11 NKJV*

Do you see the pattern of how God's order works? Don't give me that religious response... *"Well, this is the Old Testament."* The Old Testament **is** the pattern and example of what was to come (1 Corinthian 10:4-5).

SAMUEL'S SEASON WAS ABOUT TO CHANGE!

God was about to promote Samuel from serving in the temple to becoming one of His prophets in the Kingdom. Just for thought, it was Samuel who anointed the first King of Israel and prophesied that David rise to be king.

God called to Samuel one night while he was in his bedchambers saying, "SAMUEL." Samuel got up and walked all the way through the temple to Eli's bed chamber and asked what he wanted. Three times this occurred. All the while it wasn't Eli calling but God. Why did he keep going to Eli's room? Because when God speaks, He will always sound like the man of God over you!

Notice verses 8, 9 and 10, It wasn't until Eli perceived that it was the Lord calling the boy that he released Samuel to receive and respond. It was at that point Samuel was able to hear the voice of God for himself. This is the pattern... the example. If someone is trying to speak to you against, or about your future don't listen unless it's the person God has placed over you.

The same was true with Moses. The same was true with Samuel, and the same will be true with you. Don't allow the Jezebel spirit to seduce you away from the voice of your pastor. You could be heading down the road of demise and destruction.

MEMBERSHIP MUST EXPOSE AND DESTROY THIS SPIRIT

How do we destroy this evil, seducing demon? We have to raise up leadership and followers who will stand up and fight.

Elijah was no joke. He was one of the most anointed prophets of his day. No one could stand against his power and prophecies. One time, children were making fun of him because he was so different. The Bible says there were two female bears that came out of the woods and devoured them.

"Then he went up from there to Bethel; and as he was going up the road, some youths came from the city and mocked him, and said to him, "Go up, you baldhead! Go up, you baldhead!" So he turned around and looked at them, and pronounced a curse on them in the name of the Lord. And two female bears came out of the woods and mauled forty-two of the youths." 2 Kings 2:23-24 NKJV

Elijah was one of God's most anointed. However, when Jezebel sent forth her voice, he crumbled in fear and consumed by a spirit of depression.

Elijah had just called down fire on Mount Carmel and ended a three-year drought. The spirit of the Lord had fallen and King Ahab, Jezebel's husband, repented and decided to follow God. However, as soon as Ahab told Jezebel what had happened she rose up to fight even harder. This demon doesn't go away easily (1 King 18).

When Jezebel received the news she sent a word to Elijah...

"And Ahab told Jezebel all that Elijah had done, also how he had executed all the prophets with the sword. Then Jezebel sent a messenger to Elijah, saying, ' So let the gods do to me, and more also, if I do not make your life as the life of one of them by tomorrow about this time.' And when he saw that, he arose and ran for his life, and went to Beersheba, which belongs to Judah, and left his servant there." 1 Kings 19:1-3 NKJV

She decided she was going to kill the man of God. What happened to this powerful prophet? He didn't stand and fight her. He fled to the hills, wishing he could die. Elijah became so depressed over this confrontation, he actually begged God to kill him. Jezebel had never laid her hand on him, but her voice and words did more damage than if she would have struck him with a sword.

"But he himself went a day's journey into the wilderness, and came and sat down under a broom tree. And he prayed that he might die, and said, "It is enough! Now, Lord, take my life, for I am no better than my fathers!" 1 Kings 19:4 NKJV

Imagine how many leaders have been driven to the cave of depression, apathy and the spirit and mind-set of, "Why bother? Why try anymore? God, come and take me now."

This is exactly what this spirit does; it isolates to

eradicate. If Jezebel could do this to Elijah, what can she do to us? Let me give you some advice... You have to come out of the cave. When you are in the cave of depression, you develop tunnel vision, and all you see is what's at the mouth of your cave. You lose perspective and can't see the bigger picture.

God had to call into the cave and command Elijah to come out and see that his ministry wasn't over. He was about to become greater and stronger.

He was going to anoint others to excel beyond himself. God let His prophet know that He had assigned three men to judge those who were in disobedience to God's laws. He was told to go and anoint Hazael, King of Assyria, Jehu, King of Israel and a predecessor, named Elisha.

"Then the Lord said to him: "Go, return on your way to the Wilderness of Damascus; and when you arrive, anoint Hazael as king over Syria. Also you shall anoint Jehu the son of Nimshi as king over Israel. And Elisha the son of Shaphat of Abel Meholah you shall anoint as prophet in your place. It shall be that whoever escapes the sword of Hazael, Jehu will kill; and whoever escapes the sword of Jehu, Elisha will kill." 1 Kings 19:15-18 NKJV

Those who King Hazael didn't kill, King Jehu destroyed, and those who King Jehu missed Elisha killed. God has a hatred for those who cause the man or woman of God stress and unrest - that sends them running into a cave of despair and depression. This can cause men and women of God to question their calling.

"When they went from one nation to another, And from one kingdom to another people, He permitted no man to do them wrong; Yes, He rebuked kings for their sakes, Saying, "Do not touch My anointed ones, And do My prophets no harm." 1 Chronicles 16:20-22 NKJV

God will deal with those who cause division in His church

and church leadership, just as He dealt with Korah and those in the book of Numbers for speaking up against Moses (Numbers 16:31:22.) God allowed the earth to open and swallowed them up. Today God will turn these kinds of people over to themselves; He opens them up for attack. They destroy themselves from within.

"Now I urge you, brethren, note those who cause divisions and offenses, contrary to the doctrine which you learned, and avoid them. For those who are such do not serve our Lord Jesus Christ, but their own belly, and by smooth words and flattering speech deceive the hearts of the simple. For your obedience has become known to all. Therefore I am glad on your behalf; but I want you to be wise in what is good, and simple concerning evil. And the God of peace will crush Satan under your feet shortly." Romans 16:17-20 NKJV

JEHU'S REACTION

What was the first thing King Jehu did? He rode with his army straight to Jezebel's castle. He wasn't going there to make a treaty; he went there to kill her and destroy this wicked and perverse spirit.

"Now when Jehu had come to Jezreel, Jezebel heard of it; and she put paint on her eyes and adorned her head, and looked through a window." 2 Kings 9:30

As Jezebel saw the clouds of the horsemen rising over the horizon, she commenced to dress herself and adorn her body to seduce another king. God had rejected King Ahab, and Jezebel knew it. This spirit is not loyal. She immediately released Ahab and set the stage to seduce another.

This is exactly what this spirit does in the church. It moves from leader to leader, church to church and its goal is to seduce for control.

Jezebel was hanging out of her window. I can only imagine that she had pulled up the hem of her dress to show off her legs; hoping to gain the look and attention of another king. I can just imagine the smug look on her face as she swung her leg out the window waiting to set her hook; to catch her prey in a web of seduction and deceit.

King Jehu had another agenda. He did not go to be seduced; he was riding under the banner of the prophet Elijah with a command from God. It was to kill her, strike her down and destroy this controlling spirit.

*"Then, as Jehu entered at the gate, she said, "Is it peace Zimri, murderer of your master?" And he looked up at the window, and said, "**Who is on my side**? Who?" 2 Kings 9:331-32*

This scripture helped me realize that it's not leadership that is going to destroy this spirit. Jehu had no words with Jezebel, nor did he even enter her castle to engage in this fight. This could have put him at risk to be contaminated by her beguiling nature, just as Eve was in the Garden of Eden. Don't, for one moment, believe that you can sit down with this spirit and negotiate its change. It can't be done, trust me!

Jehu called out in the house of Jezebel... **"IS THERE ANYONE WHO IS ON MY SIDE?"** Jehu wanted to know if there was anyone in the house who hadn't been affected and poisoned by this witch's seduction and given into the voice of this insurrectionist? You see, this problem can't be addressed and handled by those in the house leadership. It is the commitment and loyalty of the people who need to expose and drive this enemy out.

*"So two or three eunuchs looked out at him. Then he said, "**Throw her down**." So they threw her down, and some of her blood spattered on the wall and on the horses; and he trampled her underfoot. And when he had gone in, he ate and drank." Kings 9:30-37 NKJV*

When the eunuchs looked out of the window on the other side of Jezebel, they told him that they were on his side. *"We are on the Lord's side."* Jehu commanded the comment to be proven saying, *"**If you are on my side, if you are loyal to the Lord, then throw that woman down at my feet. Throw her from the window, kick her out of the house and destroy her.**"*

What is a eunuch? They are men who have been castrated so that they cannot be seduced by the opposite sex. Eunuchs were assigned to take care of the queen's chambers because there was no fear of them having a sexual relationship with her.

The reproductive organ in the spiritual body is the ear. *"**So then faith cometh by hearing, and hearing by the word of God.**" Romans 10:17*

In the spiritual body, eunuchs are those who have dedicate themselves to the work and protection of leadership. Remember the ear is the spiritual reproductive organ. Spiritual Eunuchs are those who have circumcised their ears and altered their life so that they are unable to be seduced by the Jezebel spirit. They are the ones who can and will expose it, destroy it and throw it out of the house of God.

We need spiritual eunuchs to stand up and be counted. How about you? Are you one of those who want to become altered for Christ so that Jezebel can't use words to beguile you against the church and the man or woman of God?

*"Now I beseech you, brethren, **mark them** which cause divisions and offences contrary to the doctrine which ye have learned; and avoid them. For they that are such serve not our Lord Jesus Christ, but their own belly; and by good words and fair speeches deceive the hearts of the simple." Romans 16:17-18*

*"Brethren, be followers together of me, and **mark them** which walk so as ye have us for an example. (For many walk, of whom I have told you often, and now tell you even weeping,*

that they are the enemies of the cross of Christ: Whose end is destruction, whose God is their belly, and whose glory is in their shame, who mind earthly things.)" Philippians 3:17-19 KJV

People who enter our churches with a hidden agenda are not there to promote the gospel, and they aren't about Jesus. They have sat among us to do harm to the body of Christ.

The Bible is clear for us, as sheep, to **mark them;** the word "**mark**" in the Greek means to take aim, to box them in as one who is taking aim to shoot. It gives the meaning to take a picture of them and show their faces to everyone in the church. Why? So they can be avoided. Stay away from these kinds of people because they will do more harm in your mind than good. Run... a good run will always be better than a bad stand.

These insurrectionists are too smooth to out talk; you will eventually be persuaded to her way of thinking. Remember, this spirit moves more in women than it does in men, but that doesn't mean a man can't operate in this spirit.

BREAK COVENANT WITH THESE PEOPLE

Continuing in fellowship with these controlling and disloyal spirits can cause you to walk in their curse. This spirit has the power of masking and deceiving right down to its very appearance. It can take on many different looks or forms. You may feel like you don't need to break covenant with these people. You may have feelings that can be deceptive in your own mind. Below are a few.

DECEPTIONS TO LOOK FOR

1. *I can handle it*. Even Superman had his kryptonite. Charm is powerful and deceptive (see Proverbs 31:30).
2. *I am special to them.* They prey upon our insecurities and need for acceptance. *"And so it was, whenever*

anyone came near to bow down to him, that he would put out his hand and take him and kiss him." 2 Samuel 15:5

3. ***They are my friends***. You may be thinking that your friendship with them will not affect your connection to your local church, but it will! If you lay with dogs you will get fleas!

4. ***They love God so why should we judge them?*** If they really loved God they would not break God's government or talk and manipulate the way they do. They love themselves; not the things of God.

5. ***I can help them.*** Those operating in this spirit think they are helping you, so how are you helping them? You are going to have to correct them to help them, but you will be cut off as soon as you tell them they are wrong.

Many of us at one time have had false notions that we can restore them back into the kingdom. The enemy thrives on that sentiment. It gives him a greater road of influence, take advantage of and shipwreck you. Their main purpose is advancing their agenda. ***"Reject a divisive man after the first and second admonition." Titus 3:10***

NOTE: Deception means that you don't know you are being deceived. We think we have more discernment than we do. We forget we are dealing with a demonic spirit. Their purpose is to come against God's established authority and seek to divide His kingdom.

David had such feelings. He loved Absalom so much that he believed he could help him and eventually restore him back to the kingdom. David decided to give him mercy where God had already established His laws. *Never rewrite your theology to accommodate your tragedies.* You will cause more crisis.

7 REACTIONS THAT CREATED DAVID'S CRISIS

1. His feelings outweighed God's laws...
2. Feeling that he had to prove his compassion to others to the point of running his own kingdom and ignoring the laws of God...
3. Because of sin in David's life, He was able to over look his son's sins. He tolerated his enemy and wouldn't confront it...
4. His feelings of rejection outweighed his law of reasoning...
5. His failure as a father caused his failure as a King...
6. David's own fear of rejection caused him to love the wrong people. He loved them that hated him and hated those that loved him...
7. His lust outweighed his loyalty to his assignment.

ROOT ALWAYS PRODUCES FRUIT

I believe the number one root that produces the fruit of disloyalty is envy! Envy begins when I am not content in what I have or what I am doing. It is the inner feeling that we don't measure up. When I am not content with what I have, I can be assured I won't be content with what I want.

> "Envy is the pain and distress you feel over someone else's success!"

When I use deceit and dissension to get what I want, I can be sure that I am operating in the spirit of an insurrectionist.

The dictionary defines envy as, *"the painful or resentful awareness of an advantage enjoyed by another joined with a desire to possess the same advantage."*

FACTS ABOUT ENVY:
1. *Envy will not be grateful for what it has.*

2. *Envy won't celebrate the success of others.*
3. *Envy is never secure in itself.*
4. *Envy will never stop comparing itself to what others have and do.*
5. *Envy cannot stop competing with those who have more and do more.*
6. *Envy will never be content because of its internal issues.*
7. *Envy stops the flow of worship in people.*
8. *Envy causes bitterness and unforgiveness.*
9. *Envy is evil.*

*"Now the works of the flesh are evident, which are: adultery, fornication, uncleanness, lewdness, idolatry, sorcery, hatred, contentions, jealousies, outbursts of wrath, selfish ambitions, dissensions, heresies, **envy**, murders, drunkenness, revelries, and the like; of which I tell you beforehand, just as I also told you in time past, that those who practice such things will not inherit the kingdom of God." Galatians 5:19-21 NKJV*

Envy is empowered by imbedded bitterness. Bitterness is when people resent the fact that God has given something to another instead of them. Absalom's greatest sin was envy. Envy caused Esau to become bitter over Jacob.

Envy is developed by a self-seeking mind-set. Self-seekers always create strife and division. Strife means friction. Some call it self-ambition. Envy is fueled and maintained by a self-seeking, self-ambitious person.

Envy always speaks the loudest. It is boastful! Envy is rooted in pride. Pride leads to a boastful and bragging spirit. Envy is revealed when we feel the need to always talk about our own merits and accomplishments more than wanting to hear about someone else's. Strife is motivated by envy. It occurs when envy is present. A spirit of strife is the fruit of envy in the heart.

"For where envy and self-seeking exist, confusion and every evil thing are there." James 3:16-17 NKJV

The answer to overcoming the spirit of envy is found in James 4:1-3. *"Where do wars and fights come from among you? Do they not come from your desires for pleasure that war in your members? You lust and do not have. You murder and covet and cannot obtain. You fight and war. Yet, you do not have because you do not ask. You ask and do not receive, because you ask amiss, that you may spend it on your pleasures."*

SEVEN WEAPONS TO STOP ENVY

1. **A PURE MIND:** A mind free from defilement.
2. **A PEACEABLE MIND:** A mind free from contention and debate.
3. **A GENTLE MIND:** A mind that is kind, courteous and considerate of others.
4. **A TEACHABLE MIND:** A mind that is willing to listen, change and grow. The opposite of being stubborn.
5. **A MERCIFUL MIND:** A mind that is free from judging others. A mind that is full of grace. Mercy is a seed.
6. **AN IMPARTIAL MIND:** A mind free from prejudices. It is impartial and doesn't play favorites.
7. **A TRANSPARENT MIND:** A mind free from masks. They are transparent; what you see is who they really are.

Document Your Thoughts

CHAPTER FOUR

THE PORTRAIT OF THE
SPIRIT OF CONTROL

*J*know firsthand what it's like to be under a spirit of control. My life was filled with fear when I was younger. I was afraid of those who walked the hallways of my school, picking on guys who were smaller and different that wouldn't fight back. I was also afraid of failing if I tried and didn't succeed... afraid of not being loved or not being good enough.

These fears and the betrayal of being molested as a child, caused me to have some deep and serious wounds. These wounds caused me to second-guess myself.

I was a breeding ground for the controlling spirit to enter and sow his seeds of control into my life.

Thank God I have been healed, and I am confident and ready to take on my challenges. This healing came through years of mentorship and facing reality; not hiding in the shadows of lies and false realities. When I came clean with myself and God I began to heal.

8 SIGNS OF WHAT THE SPIRIT OF CONTROL LOOKS LIKE!

1. *They focus on themselves and not on the people.* They have an all-about-me attitude. Ego plays a big part in stimulating this mind-set.
2. *They are continually reminding people of their own authority—because it isn't based on genuine Godly character, their message or their lifestyle.* This is the core of the Jezebel spirit: **false authority.**
3. *If you mention a problem, then you become the problem.* You are accused of causing problems, not simply exposing them. They love to point fingers at others to hide and mask their own weaknesses.
4. *They are constantly taking a loyalty test.* Loyalty is demanded by them; loyalty to them instead of to

Christ. Often, repercussions will be threatened if you leave or do not follow their agenda.

5. *They use secrecy, surprises and suspense to create chaos and confusion*. They are "**the only ones who know**." You have no access to the "truths" they receive. People hide what is inappropriate, not what is appropriate. The Jezebel spirit will go to great lengths to avoid being honest, open and *transparent.* Although they will state those characteristics as being virtues that they possess.

6. *They teach unbalanced doctrines. (i.e. prophecy, biblical law or esoteric methods of biblical interpretation and spiritual methods) to the exclusion of the whole counsel of God.* This validates the group's claim of special status. There cannot be a biblically balanced presentation of the word of God when there is a Jezebel spirit in control of a group. It would defeat their efforts at manipulating and intimidating (by twisting scriptures) to control the people.

7. *They run from and will fight any source of correction.* They will do whatever they can to water-down pure truth to force their lie to become their truth. They put on an act that they have been attacked and can't believe that you have questioned their loyalty. Watch out! This person will try to destroy you behind your back in the next season.

8. *They will insist on being promoted and question why you haven't discerned that they are anointed to lead.* They will act as if they have the organization as their focus, but in reality they are out to build their own connection to those you have spent time building and training.

TECHNIQUES USED FOR CONTROL

1. **EXCESS FLATTERY**... We all want to think we're special, and respond readily to a "special" group of people who are considered to be "insiders." We all want to be a part of the "elite" group. Controlling spirits of Jezebel are more than willing to accommodate that desire. The Jezebel spirit will appear to be a loving and gracious person; oozing and dripping with flattery on those occasions when it best serves their purpose.

2. **A PROMISE TO GIVE YOU A POSITION OF AUTHORITY**... There is a follow-up on the flattery by urging you to use your "unique personal talents" to guide and teach others. The Jezebel spirit is skilled at prophesying great things about you; which you attribute to the Holy Spirit endorsing your (sometimes repressed or hidden) personal desires to be in authority. Having toyed with the idea of eventually becoming a great leader and servant for God, this type of false prophecy is very heady, exhilarating, influential and motivating.

3. **A POSITION OF GREAT AUTHORITY OVER YOU IS ASSUMED**... They will contact you again and again to try to get you to attend some sort of meeting, party or other special event and use other socially manipulative tactics in an effort to recruit you into the group—all for your own good, of course. Without continuing to add members to their little personal cult, the Jezebel spirit will lose its sphere of influence quickly.

4. **YOU WILL BE LED TO RESPOND TO QUESTIONS WITH THE ANSWERS THEY WANT YOU TO GIVE TO CONFIRM THEIR AUTHORITY**... This can often be in the form of group psychology. They continue to flatter you, while leading you through a hidden agenda and making it appear as

though the answers you gave meant that you strongly supported their point of view on your own free will. The controlling Jezebel spirit derives false authority from those who don't see through this manipulative ploy. Having planted the idea in your head that you will become another Moses (or equivalent) for God, the Jezebel spirit will continue to attempt to assert their false authority over you in what they consider to be clever, non-intrusive, subtle techniques. **THE FORMER FLATTERY WILL BE USED AGAINST YOU.** Now disappointed, in contrast with wild praise, the perceived loss of esteem, such a response can serve as a powerful force motivating dissenters to "get with the program." They will let you know in so many words that you "owe" them for your blessings. We don't like to disappoint those who initially claim to be impressed with us, especially when they assume a position of authority over us and claim to have "selected" us for membership in some supposed special group.

The Jezebel spirit might also express disappointment in you; and lead you to believe that you have disappointed God by your failure to conduct yourself as an up-and-coming powerful religious leader.

5. **THE RULES OF THE GAME WILL BE CHANGED EARLY ON, WITH NO WARNING, AND PROCEED AS THOUGH NOTHING UNUSUAL HAS HAPPENED...** Such "bait and switch" tactics are typical of those who attempt to recruit others into positions of authority. At this stage, most people will slowly begin to internalize the point of view of the "Jezebel" and make the act of repressing any doubt; believing them to be fundamental components of their own thought process.

The Jezebel spirit knows the power of the human ego. It feeds your ego the food it needs to become self-centered and focused on having the "spiritual authority" you think God wants you to have. This is analogous to building castles in the sand.

6. **THEY WILL CONTRADICT THEMSELVES MANY TIMES THROUGHOUT THE COURSE OF YOUR RELATIONSHIP.** They will cover their tracks by repeatedly verbalizing their stated objections toward the very tactics they used to manipulate you from the start. They believe your view of yourself as an independent, free-thinking person, would most likely make it difficult for you to fully recognize the many ways in which they were controlling the underlying agenda from the start.

Controlling spirits of Jezebel are very clever in continuing to make you think that you are in control of your own life. In fact, you are under the worst kind of bondage of one human to another. This is another way the Jezebel spirit converts you into thinking that you too, have spiritual authority, which of course, is really false authority.

7. **THE DESIRE TO AVOID FEELINGS OF DISILLUSIONMENT AND ISOLATION...** This may be one of the most powerful factors motivating those who choose to remain connected to the spirit of a manipulator; even after it appears obvious that the extraordinary hopes and desires they had when they first joined a particular group are never likely to be fulfilled.

This can occur because the hopes for relationships and significance were considered part of the prize.

The controlling spirit knows that your desire to preserve your own *illusions of fulfillment of your hopes and desires will override your logical* analysis of their controlling Jezebel spirit tactics. Logic is a motivator, but the controlling spirit knows that **emotions are much more powerful and will override logic**. They also know that enthusiasm on their part reinforces your emotions beyond anything else they can do.

THE CONTROLLING SPIRIT

There is a distinction between a **spirit of control** and having diligence to fulfill ones responsibilities. Those who are born leaders have the tendency to micromanage and appear to be controlling; however, this is not a spirit.

Many people confuse the two and rationalize their controlling spirit by saying something like, "Well, I'm just trying to live up to my responsibilities." It is so vital for each of us to understand the difference and discern when it is a spirit and not just leadership gifts.

Living up to your responsibilities simply means that you work hard and diligently to fulfill those responsibilities, whether they are at home, in your family-life, at work or in any relationship you have. We have the command to be responsible, diligent and hard working at whatever we put our hands to do.

> "Discernment Is When The Spirit Is Telling You Something That Your Mind Isn't."

Things are very different with the *controlling spirit.* Controlling people work hard to manipulate other people, events and circumstances, to make things go their way. They spend their waking hours trying to figure out how to spin, engineer and manipulate situations to their advantage and gain. Controlling people get very upset and angry when things don't go their way. They are convinced that the world around them will fall apart if they are not in control; whether at home, at work or any position they are in. They must be in control to be comfortable.

They think that nothing can be done right. Nothing good can happen without their input, direction and control. Believe me when I tell you that there are people that think that even God can't do anything without them. They think that they know better than God, and that God needs their help, their input, their planning, their scheming, their ideas and plans in order for things to go the right way. They believe that their way is the only possible right way, the only proper way and beneficial way. Of course, it is always for their own best interest because they think they are the center of the universe.

The controlling spirit is the number one enemy of faith. The controlling spirit is the biggest hindrance to the work of faith in our lives. The controlling spirit can overwhelm faith and leave no room for it to operate in our lives. The controlling spirit leaves no room for individuality or freedom when it is trying to exercise control over you. The controlling spirit ruins relationship and causes headaches, loneliness, isolation and ultimately squeezes God and faith out of living. It is very grieving to the Holy Spirit.

The Holy Spirit cannot work in the life of someone with a controlling spirit because He is a gentleman. The Holy Spirit is totally blocked and stopped from operating and working in the life of a person with a controlling spirit. These people cannot come to Christ; they cannot put their faith in Christ, or trust and believe in anyone or anything **but themselves** until they are delivered from this demonic spirit.

A person with a controlling spirit worships self. Self sits on the throne of their heart and rules everything. The only perspective they can see and understand is their own. Any ideas or thoughts that are contrary to the controlling person are found to be unacceptable, and they will fight "tooth and nail" to defeat them.

People with a controlling spirit are
- Heady and intoxicating
- High-minded
- Head-strong
- Overbearing
- Merciless

- Highly Opinionated
- Selfish
- Uncaring people who struggle to have things their way against all odds.

Let's look at a scriptural example of the danger of a controlling spirit and how to be delivered from it.

"And Elisha came again to Gilgal: and there was a death in the land; and the sons of the prophets were sitting before him: and he said unto his servant, Set on the great pot, and seethe pottage for the sons of the prophets. And one went out into the field to gather herbs, and found a wild vine, and gathered thereof wild gourds his lap full, and came and shred them into the pot of pottage: for they knew them not. So they poured out for the men to eat. And it came to pass, as they were eating of the pottage, that they cried out, and said, O thou man of God, there is death in the pot. And they could not eat thereof. But he said, 'then bring meal. And he cast it into the pot;' and he said, 'Pour out for the people, that they may eat. And there was no harm in the pot." 2 Kings 4:38-41

This is a living example of how the controlling spirit fashioned intrusion into God's provision. This intrusion could have brought misery and possible death to the whole community. The person with the controlling spirit sought to improve God's plan and purpose, and such an effort can be devastating and cause death. The one with the controlling spirit not only hurts those who yield themselves to it, but families, communities and the people of God. It can also hurt the work of God.

There are three important points in this passage. First, there was a famine in the land. Most of us don't truly know or understand the full affects of famine because we haven't experienced one. Those who have visited countries or seen enough news coverage of a land in famine can at least get an idea of the terrible devastation and death it brings to many.

Be very careful in times of stress; it can be an opportunity to trust God with all of your heart, or they become windows for disaster. Stress can become a time of exercising faith in the faithfulness of God, or they can become a doorway to calamity and tragedy.

During this time, Elisha had inherited the title of "President" at the school of the prophets, or seminary. Elisha was responsible for their training and well being. The students at the seminary were **"God was, is and always will be in the miracle business."** obviously affected by the famine like everyone else in the land.

Elisha returned from a preaching mission, and checked on the community of faith he was training. After seeing the famine, he realized what was going on. So he told his servant to go and get a large pot, not a small or medium size, but a large pot and make a stew that would be enough for everyone.

Wait a minute; Elisha just learned that there was a famine in the land, so how was the servant supposed to accomplish this? Where would the servant get the food? Good question. God will always make provision for His faithful ones in tough times. God has always refreshed His righteous saints in times of disaster. He has always proved His sufficiency to His saints during times of need. God always honors those who honor Him. He will always be a light to the faithful in the midst of darkness and will always bring water out of the rock to quench the thirst of His people. He will multiply and increase the little that His faithful have. God supernaturally provided for His people through the faith of the prophet Elisha.

God was, is and always will be in the miracle business. God will never go out of the miracle business because it's a part of who He is. He is supernatural even in the midst of calamity, even in the midst of natural disaster, even in the midst of judgment and even in the midst of stressful time. God will always move on behalf of His faithful children.

There was a famine in the land of Canaan in the book of Genesis. It threatened to wipe out Jacob and all of his children. This meant that the whole nation of Israel, from who the Messiah would come, would have been wiped out. God sent Joseph to the land of Egypt ahead of time in order to spare them. *God is always ahead of time.*

God supernaturally provided light for His children when everyone in the nation of Egypt was plunged into darkness in the book of Exodus.

God supernaturally provided for the prophet Elijah when there was a famine that struck the land of Israel in the book of 1 Kings.

"For the LORD God is a sun and shield: the LORD will give grace and glory: no good thing will he withhold from them that walk uprightly." Psalm 84:11

He didn't say perfect, but "upright" which in the Hebrew means to *be undefiled, without spot, sound complete and whole.* This is all fulfilled by being washed in the blood of Jesus and being under the grace of God. It has to do with your heart's attitude, motivation and condition. God doesn't expect absolute sinless perfection from us. He knows that the only time we will be perfect is when we are face to face with Jesus and have a body just like His after the resurrection. He does want us to walk blameless before Him but don't confuse blameless with perfection.

Walking blameless is different than perfection. Walking blameless is recognizing and knowing when to repent and understanding how to repent. Walking blameless means that we are sensitive to God. This brings us immediately under conviction when we do wrong, or we are headed in the wrong direction. We don't wait, we don't delay or resist the leading of

His Spirit to change directions; and if needed, we repent to keep our fellowship with God open and alive.

Too many want to hide behind semantics and say; *"Well I confessed my sin many years ago."* *So what! Are you walking in repentance?*

Repentance is a change in lifestyle. The word actually means to turn around and go a different direction. Many churches have watered down the power of salvation and the key to eternal life. Jesus paid for our salvation by His death on the cross; however, there is a price that we must pay and a certain walk we must strive to live every day.

Westernized Christianity, and our post-modern culture, has created a god after our own thinking that fits neatly into our brain. We have created a god in our own image that conforms to our own likes and dislikes. If we don't like something God must not like it; if we like something then He must like it too. We have created a god who is obedient to our wishes as a servant. We have created a god who must desire what we desire, a god who will never judge us no matter what we do. We have created a god that we can walk away from when we don't need Him, but is expected to be there for us when we come into a hard situation. We have created a god who is helpless without us; a god of our own making. **This is the very atmosphere that creates a controlling spirit...**

The greatest tragedy in the world is the one among God's people because they have ceased to believe that God is supernatural and in the supernatural business. Most people who go to church don't believe that Jesus is Lord of all and sitting on the throne of the universe. They try to bring God down to their image and make Him like man. They even make Him their servant instead of giving Him His rightful place as Lord in their lives; submitting their lives to His Lordship to honor, please and serve Him. They serve self, honor self, please self and worship self instead. They don't realize this because they are deceived. Our hearts are so easily deceived. This is why God spoke the words of Jeremiah 17:9, *"The heart is deceitful above all things, and desperately wicked: who can know it?"*

In the midst of this famine, God supernaturally provided for this community through the faith of Elisha. Elisha told the servant to get a big pot and make a stew for the people. So he brought the big pot and made this stew. It would have been great if the story ended here; everything went as planned and all were provided for and praised God. However, God's miracles are never enough for the controlling spirit. They always have to improve on God's provision and faithfulness and modify His plan. They love to get the credit for self. In verse 39, one of them went out and found a wild vine, gathered some herbs and gourds and put them into his cloak thinking it would improve and add to the recipe.

"And one went out into the field to gather herbs, and found a wild vine, and gathered thereof wild gourds his lap full, and came and shred them into the pot of pottage: for they knew them not." II Kings 4:39

This person knew that Elisha's faith had provided for them. This didn't stop him from trying to help so there would be more food. He tossed the stuff into the pot, probably thinking how great a job he was doing by adding the additional ingredients. He probably thought he was doing them a favor and couldn't wait until they all said how wonderful it was so he could take the credit. You know the kind, *"Well, I know God provides, but not without my help."* Do you see the humor in this? **If not, then you have not dealt with the controlling spirit**. If you are gritting your teeth and grimacing over this, rather than seeing the humor, then you have not begun to be delivered from the spirit of control. Faith cannot operate in your life as long as the spirit of control has control over you.

This guy just couldn't stand for God to do something without his help. He could not accept just receiving from the hand of God. He couldn't accept just being a child of God at the table; he wanted to be the father, the provider. **This guy couldn't accept just being the servant**; he wanted to be the master. He couldn't accept being a guest of God; he wanted to be the chief and the host. He wanted to improve upon God's recipe.

Be careful when you try to improve upon God's provision. Un-be-known to this man, he had just added poison and death to God's pot of provision. What he had just added to God's miracle was a disaster.

> **"Never Try To Improve On God's Recipe for Change."**

What he just added to God's work of faith was neutralizing the miracle of God's provision. Listen, all of God's big helpers; God loves you, but He wants you to give Him room in your life to work in and through you. God wants you to meet the condition of His promises. God wants you to trust Him with all your being. That's it and that's all.

Cain didn't like the idea of offering the animal sacrifice and shedding the blood the way God had taught Adam and Eve. Instead, he decided he would come to God his way, on his own terms. As a result, he was filled with anger and jealousy when God would not accept his sacrifice. It was his own fault not Abel's. However, Cain killed Abel instead of seeing his own failure and admitting his rebellion and disobedience as the reason for God's rejection. It was **Cain who had poisoned the pot,** poisoning his heart and bringing physical death to his brother and spiritual death to himself.

The sons of Aaron, Moses' brother, wanted to worship God their own way. **They poisoned the pot**.

The sons of Eli, the priest, decided to worship God their way and brought defeat to the nation of Israel and their own destruction. **They poisoned the pot.**

King Saul offered God a sacrifice His way, not waiting for the prophet Samuel, but choosing to get out of the will of God and thus caused disaster to the nation of Israel. **He poisoned the pot**.

In Acts, a couple named Ananias and Sapphira took control by trying to deceive the church. They **poisoned the pot and brought death upon themselves.**

Anytime we try to do things our way instead of God's way, we poison the pot.

We hinder the blessings of God and stop them dead in their tracks. It's a dangerous thing to operate your business your way, your ministry your way, bring up your children your way, serve God your way or to do anything your way that is contrary to God's way. These things will always poison the pot.

The good news is in verse 41 of I Kings 4. *"But he said, 'Then bring meal.' And he cast it into the pot; and he said, 'Pour out for the people, that they may eat.' And there was no harm in the pot."*

Elisha told them to put flour in the pot, and the poison was neutralized. What is this all about? What is this saying to us? In the scriptures, flour is a type of the resurrected Christ.

Flour is the product of crushing and milling the grain of wheat. In John chapter twelve, Jesus said that unless a grain of wheat falls into the ground and die, it will not produce a harvest. He was speaking of Himself. Jesus was the flour taken to the pot of death, and then brought forth back to life. Jesus is the flour that neutralizes the poison of death and helplessness. Jesus is the flour that has put an end to man's efforts. Jesus is the flour that put an end to man's desire to be saved by his own good works.

- Jesus is the flour that ended the power of ceremonial law.
- Jesus is the flour that raised us up from death.
- Jesus is the flour that saves us from ourselves.
- Jesus is the flour that prevents disaster that is caused by the controlling spirit.

The resurrected Jesus Christ is the only One who

can give you power to nullify the power of the controlling spirit so you can do His work. The question is, will you confess to Him and then let Him take over? Will you let the flour come into the pot of your life and neutralize the poison of the controlling spirit?

The spirit of control will stop the miracle of blessing and provision that God has for you every time. If you are facing this spirit, ask God to deliver you from it today so that you can be free to serve Him and do His will instead of your own.

CHAPTER FIVE

Loyalty Is A Rare Gift

*"...And give my son Solomon a **loyal heart** to keep your commandments and Your testimonies and Your statutes, to do all these things, and to build the temple for which I have made provision."1 Chronicles 29:19 NKJV*

$\mathcal{I}$n this scripture, David is praying over the next King of Israel, his son Solomon. David asked the Lord to give his son a loyal heart. It is necessary for membership and leadership to walk in loyalty.

The dictionary defines loyalty as; *faithful to the constituted authority of one's country. Faithful to those persons, ideals, etc. that one is under obligation to defend, support, or be true to relating to, or indicating loyalty.*

Loyalty is faithfulness to hold fast to your commitments even after circumstances have changed.

The greatest thing missing in our churches from the pulpit to the pew is **loyalty!**

Look around. Watch how many people will leave your church within a year. They come in and want to be connected, then all of a sudden cool off, and show disinterest in the church and what it is doing. Their attendance starts wavering; their attitude starts changing. Suddenly they are talking about the pastor, the leaders or someone in the church they don't like. This once loyal and fired up member is now walking in a spirit of anger and bitterness.

We must strive to stop this spirit of disloyalty from destroying what men and women of God are trying to build for the Kingdom of God.

I was sitting in a room with some great men of God once. One of these men was talking about a certain person who had been with him for years and then suddenly rose up and attacked him. The other preacher sitting beside me said, "I tell you what; **loyalty is a rare gift to have around you."** I do believe this to be true.

Loyalty is measured through time... There are many people around us that may appear to be loyal; however, loyalty is measured by time. Loyalty is abiding and remaining even when things around you have changed. In my book, *"God's Unwavering Faithfulness"*, I touched on the subject of a servant worker verses a servant attitude.

> **"The Proof of Loyalty is measured through time..."**

SERVANT WORKER VERSES SERVANT ATTITUDE

The heart of a servant is different than that of someone who just fills a servant's role. Many times, I've seen people that will try to serve leaders because they see an end to a means not because they are servants. They know that by serving they can get close to the leader to make connections for their future. The truth is that no one who enters serving with this agenda is going to remain loyal. Expect them to rise up against you as soon as they have obtained all they need. They are not about you or what you're doing. They are not interested in what you've learned. They are only interested in what you have earned. In case you don't understand... **THEY WANT YOUR STUFF!**

How do I know that you are a servant? *When I treat you like a servant and you don't become angry or agitated with me.* There is a big difference in doing the work of a servant and having the heart of a servant.

Don't allow people to become servants in your life until they have passed the test of time. Time will prove them... Time will reveal their motives... Time exposes hidden agenda's. I encourage you to move quickly and swiftly away from them if they begin to show disloyal attributes.

Remember, those you allow around you who could be the deciding factor to your season, good or bad. Don't allow wrong people to connect to you. They could be walking in a disobedient lifestyle. They could have left their last season with a crisis that they haven't taken care of. Now they have connected you to their consequences.

Jonah's disobedience affected everyone on the boat with him. Jonah was running from God and God's instruction. Halfway through the trip a great storm appeared and began to sink the ship. Here is where it gets "hairy." The people begin to throw their things from the ship; believing something they had – or had not done- was causing this crisis. However, Jonah knew that it was not *what* they had on the ship, but *who* was on the ship that was causing all their problems. Jonah told them to throw him overboard, and their storm would be over.

How many could be living in a storm right now that wasn't scheduled for their life, but they allowed wrong people around? Now they are experiencing their problems.

QUALIFY THOSE YOU WANT TO CONNECT TO YOU

Loyalty is a decision of the will, not an emotional response of the heart. People decide to be loyal. Loyalty is not an emotion. You don't feel loyalty, you decide to be loyal. It's a decision of the will. If loyalty were based on feelings, then even Jesus Himself may have become disloyal. I can tell you that when you are serving a leader there will be times where your feelings and emotions will be strained beyond comprehension. The moment you let your emotions have a voice you will begin to be deceived by the enemy or wrong people. That voice will make declarations such as, *"You're not appreciated... no one ever notices your effort and your willingness to serve."* You will start developing the "what about me" syndrome. It happens all of the time...no one cares... no one loves me... no one notices me... and the list goes on and on.

If you haven't made the commitment to follow, the decision to be loyal, to remain, to stay faithful and abide, you will most assuredly make the wrong decision. Then you will leave a place where God may have planned to bless you beyond measure.

Many have left my ministry before it was their time to leave. Don't misunderstand me, some needed to leave, but there were others that left because their feelings were hurt, or they developed a misunderstanding. As a result, these people left with a wrong attitude. They were not sent by God. They just went. Those who are sent by God do great things for God; those who "*went*" somewhere usually find themselves in a nomadic state of living. They just keep wondering around from one place to another trying to fit in but never seem to be able to. I believe those who leave a season the wrong way never develop the correct mind-set to be *sent* to the next. Don't be fooled. The churches are full of such nomadic people. These people will always be disloyal.

I had a family that came to The Favor Center wounded and hurt. Their marriage was about to end in divorce... their children were mad and bitter over what had happened in their home. I made a mistake because I didn't qualify why they were at The Favor Center or what had happened at their last church. I spent time counseling and praying with them, but as soon as their marriage began to heal, they did a one-hundred eighty degree turn on me. They seemed full of leadership skills that would be a valuable help to the ministry in the beginning of our relationship. What a deception! They had what I call the *entry of the palace but content of a hut*. To make a long story short, they left in the night and moved on to another church to try to do damage there. I later found out they had left one church because they became mad at the senior pastor. Not only did they leave, but they caused a church split and tried to start another church. During the season of starting another church, their marriage became strained and the wife began to be unfaithful. As a result, they lost the church. Then they entered my ship (church) as a Jonah. I'm telling you Pastor, qualify everybody. Trust, but verify. This is my motto from now on.

"**Trust but Verify!**"

All I needed to do was ask questions. We have been so

conditioned to receive everybody in our churches that we are allowing Jezebel spirits to come in and destroy all we have worked for. This is not what we, as leaders, are to do. We are to be qualifiers.

The nickname for pastor is shepherd. What do shepherds really do? They lead their sheep to green pastures. They anoint their heads with oil. They sit on the high place and watch for wolves that might be trying to sneak into the sheep fold to do bodily harm. What does a shepherd do when he sees a wolf? He kills it. This is for the protection of the whole herd not just one. We need to rise up and become sheep inspectors; making sure wolves haven't tried to mask themselves as sheep.

Loyalty is staying in submission after agreement ends. When does submission begin? Submission begins after agreement has ended. The truest test of loyalty is when you can stay connected even when you really don't agree with what's happening around you. The church will grow and become healthier if you will just walk through the season of confusion. Allow time for the leader to build their plan.

Loyalty is when you line up in agreement to the vision. We all like to use the word submission, especially when it relates to marriage. The truth is that no husband really wants a submissive wife; he really wants a wife who is in agreement. The same is true in ministry. Men and women of God become tired and frustrated

> "Lack of loyalty is one of the major causes of failure in every walk of life." Napoleon Hill

when the people walking with them are only walking in submission; constantly having to be persuaded to the vision. Those who are in agreement with the man or woman of God help take the struggle out of success. *"Behold, how good and how pleasant it is for brethren to dwell together in unity! It is like the precious oil upon the head, running down on the beard,* the beard of Aaron, Running down on the edge of his garments." Psalm 133:1-2 NKJV

Agreement is liken unto the oil.

Love doesn't necessarily mean you will be loyal. Maybe I should say human love because God's love is full of loyalty. God was faithful while we were yet sinners. Human love seems to have a weakness; as soon as the feeling is gone so is the commitment and loyalty. We are so cheap in our love and loyalty. We lack understanding of what real love and real loyalty means.

How many have stood at an altar looking into each other's eyes on their wedding day declaring their unwavering love? After some time these same people who were once in love now walk away from each other. The same couple who once said, *"I will never leave you... I will never walk away, through sickness, through death, through good times and bad times I will be here..."* are now divorcing. Their love has now turned into hate for each other. Over seventy percent of marriages end in divorce.

I say this because so many enter church confessing their love and support to the pastor; however, as easy as they entered they will eventually divorce. When they do, they will be as hateful as those same couples who pledged their everlasting love.

God's love is everlasting to everlasting.

We need to wake up and start an extensive qualification process before we give a platform and position to those who just appear to be for us. Look at this verse in John.

"They went out from us, but they were not of us; for if they had been of us, they would have continued with us; but they went out that they might be made manifest, that none of them were

of us." 1 John 2:19 NKJV

If they were of us they would have continued with us. When they left they proved they weren't of us. I have spent many days crying over those who left me and my ministry in times past. Let me clarify, not all who leave are walking in a spirit of Jezebel or out of God's will. We all understand that we can't lead everybody. Different strokes for different folks. However, many of those who leave, or have exited our lives, did so wrong; causing bodily harm to the Kingdom of God. These deep cuts and wounds can take months to heal, especially in those sheep that became prey to these wolves. There will be a day when those people will have to answer for their sins of disloyalty and dissension.

To be loyal, we must die to human love and pick up and carry the love of God in our hearts for all men.

"Hell has no weapon against a person who decides to love everybody."

I was in Detroit, Michigan with my wife to minister when God woke me up with a still small voice whispering so gently in my spirit. *"Hell has no weapon against a man who has decided to love everybody."* No man can fail when he has decided to love instead of hate. My response was, *"Lord, I don't understand. Are you telling me to love?"* The Lord impressed this upon me. *"Son you decide to love, I can't make you choose love. Love is your decision. To Love your enemies son, you are going to have to possess my love in you, which is Christ's love."* **God's love through Christ in us is the only real way to stay loyal.**

I began to cry and ask the Holy Spirit to help me to forgive; to release in my heart the offenses and wounds that I had allowed others to place there. *"Lord, You are my Healer, and no one can remove these infractions but You."* I realize now that at that moment I began to heal on the inside. So many of us are trying to fix ourselves from the outside in, but I can tell you this truth, it works better when you heal from the inside first. What's happening around us is usually a clue to what's going on in us.

WHY IS LOYALTY SO IMPORTANT?

1. **Loyalty is the principal qualification for every person who desires to minister in the body of Christ.** *"Let a man so consider us, as servants of Christ and stewards of the mysteries of God. Moreover it is required in stewards that one be found faithful." 1 Corinthians 4:1-3 NKJV*
2. **Loyalty will produce peace and safety in the local church**. Where there is no loyalty the atmosphere becomes agitated and aggressive. The rest of the church can't find water to drink because sheep won't drink in an unsafe environment.
3. ***Loyalty will allow the love of God to flow in the church***. *"A new commandment I give to you, that you love one another; as I have loved you, that you also love one another. By this all will know that you are My disciples, if you have love for one another." John 13:34-35 NKJV*
4. **Loyalty is required to have a healthy ministry.**
5. **Loyalty is required to have a long lasting and joyful ministry.**
6. ***Loyalty must be present in our lives*** **in order to reap our full reward**. *"But you are those who have continued with Me in My trials. And I bestow upon you a kingdom, just as My Father bestowed one upon Me, that you may eat and drink at My table in My kingdom, and sit on thrones judging the twelve tribes of Israel." Luke 22:28-31 NKJV*

Document Your Thoughts

CHAPTER SIX

EIGHT STAGES OF DISLOYALTY

*"Beware of false prophets, who come to you in sheep's clothing,
but inwardly they are ravenous wolves. You will know them
by their fruits. Do men gather grapes from thorn bushes or figs
from thistles? Even so, every good tree bears good fruit, but a
bad tree bears bad fruit. A good tree cannot bear bad fruit,
nor can a bad tree bear good fruit. Every tree that does not
bear good fruit is cut down and thrown into the fire. Therefore
by their fruits you will know them."*
Matthew 7:15-20 NKJV

*M*any start out in our churches excited about what
God is going to do with them in their newly found church. After
a while, those once enthusiastic people begin to wax cold and
start talking about the church and leadership they were once so
in love with.

Disloyalty is the number one killer in most churches and
ministries. It is the curse of disloyalty that ruins many
marriages. The faithful become unfaithful. I have a problem
with those who call themselves my
friend, or say they are connected with
me, but sit in my enemy's presence
and feel comfortable. How can you
say you're with me, sitting at the table

> **"Sometimes
> ministry just can't
> be nice."**

with those who believe I am not good enough to lead them?
Disloyal people are worse than a thousand demons.

HOW TO DEAL WITH THE SPIRIT OF DISLOYALTY

1. Become discerning of spirits that need to be corrected in
   leadership. Discernment is when the spirit tells you
   something the mind won't.

2. Proper role modeling. If the rest of the sheep see you hobnobbing with the disloyal, then they will think it is okay to do also.
3. Have a sheep-dog mentality. Protect the sheep from being kissed (bitten). Remember, wolves don't come dressed as wolves, but as sheep.
4. Stop tolerating their antics. Put an end to the disloyal spirit. Immediately fire disloyalty... It's a heart issue. They always cry when they are caught. Don't mistake their tears of exposure as tears of repentance.
5. Don't give them a place in the life of the body.
6. Avoid promoting people until their true character is proven.
7. Mark those who cause division and avoid them. Teach the people in your church to do the same. *"Now I urge you, brethren, note those who cause divisions and offenses, contrary to the doctrine which you learned, and avoid them. For those who are such do not serve our Lord Jesus Christ, but their own belly, and by smooth words and flattering speech deceive the hearts of the simple."* Romans 16:17-18
8. Pray for them. *"Woe to you when all men speak well of you, For so did their fathers to the false prophets. But I say to you who hear: Love your enemies, do well to those who hate you, bless those who curse you, and pray for those who spitefully use you."* Luke 6:26-28
9. Leave vengeance to the Lord. Their own pride will bring them down.

STAGE ONE: THE INDEPENDENT STAGE

This is the stage when the rules of the group no longer apply. These are those who think that they are so indispensable that they can do what they want, say what they want and come and go when they feel like it.

They are late to most meetings. Tardiness is silent rebellion. They are never consistent on anything they commit too. Oh, they will be the ones who shout the loudest. Always standing and saying "Amen" to you while you are preaching; especially if you are preaching about the things others are doing.

They do what they want and not what they are told. They interpret your instructions instead of following them. They are those who you wish would leave, but never do. They will stick around until they have poisoned everyone else.

They will always be the ones who speak against what you are demanding of others. They are always full of excuses. Expect stage two when you try to correct them and mentor them.

STAGE TWO: THE OFFENSE STAGE

Jesus was asked by his disciples what would the end be like and what would be the sign of His coming?

*"Now as He sat on the Mount of Olives, the disciples came to Him privately, saying, "Tell us, when these things will be? And what will be the sign of your coming, and of the end of the age?" And Jesus answered and said to them: "Take heed that no one deceives you. For many will come in My name, saying, 'I am the Christ,' and will deceive many. And you will hear of wars and rumors of wars. See that you are not troubled; for all these things must come to pass, but the end is not yet. For nation will rise against nation, and kingdom against kingdom. And there will be famines, pestilences, and earthquakes in various places. All these are the beginning of sorrows. Then they will deliver you up to tribulation and kill you, and you will be hated by all nations for My name's sake. **__And then many will be offended__**, will betray one another, and will hate one another. Then many false prophets will rise up and deceive many. And because lawlessness will abound, the love of many will grow cold. But he who endures to the end shall be saved.*

And this gospel of the kingdom will be preached in all the world as a witness to all the nations, and then the end will come." Matthew 24:3-14 NKJV

When Jesus decided to talk about what the end would look like, He said there would be wars, and rumors of wars, pestilence, sickness, etc. All these have been around for a long time and these were only what the end would look like. They were not the signs of the end. The sign of the end was this... **"Many would be offended in that day... and would betray one another, and hate one another..."**

We have never in any generation seen so many people taking others to court for the most trivial and spiteful reasons. We see intolerance running rampant, and forgiveness that is superficial. We pretend to ignore what somebody did, or act like it didn't matter, but then walk away and find someone to tell all about what happened and how we were offended. ***Sadly, this is not forgiveness.***

We are such pampered, spoiled people, that we get annoyed with everything, and we feel like it is our right to say so. Sometimes we cven get more than offended; we get indignant.

"They shouldn't have done it that way. They should have had it ready. That shouldn't have been this way and that should have been that way. I don't like this."

After that process, we might even get a little resentful and start remembering ***every time*** a person, place, or thing was offensive in the past. *"It seems as though every time I go there I get offended,"* or *"they acted like that the last time,"* and *"whaa, whaa, whaa..."* (Baby!)

The spirit of offense can affect us on a daily basis. We have to choose not to allow people, words or actions to offend us. After a period of time, if you consistently build on the benefit of the doubt, tolerance, patience, understanding and you always allow for human imperfection, you will begin to enjoy the people around you and even cherish their unique differences. You may even find that you are amused at the very things that used to annoy you. Anything you do for twenty-one days consistently becomes a habit. We have to work at not being offended. It takes effort, but it is well worth it.

Can you see how this process is becoming internalized? It will evolve into a **spirit of offense** that becomes a part of who you are. Eventually it will have an external effect on your behavior and how you perceive the world around you. This is the point where your joy of life is stolen away by your own self.

In this stage, correction to those walking independently won't change them; it offends them. This offense means they become angry, hurt, resentful and begin to disconnect and become disloyal to the headship.

STAGE THREE: THE UNINVOLVED STAGE

"Cursed is he who does the work of the Lord deceitfully, And cursed is he who keeps back his sword from blood." Jeremiah 48:10NKJV

Watch out for **uninvolved** people; those who started out in the front, but now sit in the back. They never act like they're listening. They never involve themselves in conversation about your vision. When they do speak, it is always in a negative attitude about what is being done.

People who are not consistent in their attendance, giving, and work in the church have the potential of becoming a disloyal person. Never place these people in leadership because they will eventually turn on you and try to hurt those you are leading.

When you try to help these people by mentoring them or correcting them, their attitude will always be **"whatever..."** They will have a "stop bothering me" attitude.

STAGE FOUR: THE CRITICAL STAGE

The uninvolved, passive person will always turn into the critical person in your house. ***Skepticism creates the greatest loss on the earth.*** Criticism can stop the best of momentums. You must avoid those who are going to be critical of your vision and your leadership. It is at this stage when they begin to find fault.

Anything unflawed is an illusion. Everything is flawed. Nothing on the earth is perfect. No one on the earth is perfect. God left Himself out of everything on the earth so that when we connect to it, it wouldn't complete us. The only perfect source on the earth is Jesus. When these people discover your faults they will magnify them to be bigger than they really are. They do this to prove themselves to be right.

Absalom only saw David's faults. He never saw David's greatness or anointing. Absalom didn't even recognize David's mercy and love. By all rights, Absalom should've been killed for his actions against his half brother. It was David's mercy that saved him. However, Absalom was only concerned about one thing, and that was his promotion. He was critical about everything David did.

> **"Skepticism Creates The Greatest Loss On The Earth."**

Critical people love to talk to those who are complainers, especially if it is someone who is complaining about the same thing they are disconnecting from. These people forget that it was God who set the man of God in that house. When they rise up to complain they anger the Lord.

STAGE FIVE: THE POLITCAL STAGE

When someone begins to build an offense and starts to unplug themselves, they begin to complain and criticize everything they see. These people will start to build a following with those who are of the same persuasion and have the same problem. Sometimes, others will connect that didn't have any problem, but lost confidence in their leader when someone began to build doubt and questions in them.

Have you ever been driving down the interstate, put your blinker on, confident in your decision when the passenger with you says, *"Are you sure you want to take this exit?"* What happens? You immediately turn your vehicle back into traffic and look at your passenger and say... *"Yes. Why? Do you know something that I don't?"* You were confident until someone questioned your decision. That question caused you to turn back into the wrong direction and added delay to your destination. The same is true in our churches. There are those who know without a shadow of a doubt that they belong in that church, but all of a sudden someone shows up and questions their loyalty... their decision to what they were confident in. What happens? They begin to build their own criticism and skepticism.

This disloyal insurrectionist begins to politic to prove they are right.

"Now this I say lest anyone should deceive you with persuasive words. For though I am absent in the flesh, yet I am with you in spirit, rejoicing to see your good order and the steadfastness of your faith in Christ. As you therefore have received Christ Jesus the Lord, so walk in Him, rooted and built up in Him and established in the faith, as you have been taught, abounding in it with thanksgiving. Beware lest anyone cheat you through philosophy and empty deceit, according to the tradition of men, according to the basic principles of the world, and not according to Christ. For in Him dwells all the fullness of the Godhead bodily; and you are complete in Him, who is the head of all principality and power." Colossians 2:4-10 NKJV

"Now I urge you, brethren, note those who cause divisions and offenses, contrary to the doctrine which you learned, and avoid them. For those who are such do not serve our Lord Jesus Christ, but their own belly, and by smooth words and flattering speech deceive the hearts of the simple. For your obedience has

become known to all. Therefore I am glad on your behalf; but I want you to be wise in what is good, and simple concerning evil. And the God of peace will crush Satan under your feet shortly." Romans 16:17-20 NKJV

They start asking political questions to find out who they can hook and deceive into their little camp. They ask loaded questions. They disguise their real identity in questions and statements such as these.

BAITED QUESTION OR STATEMENTS

1. How did you find the service today?
2. As a Bible-based church, don't you think we should see more miracles?
3. Do you believe that the pastor's focus has changed? He seems to be over focused on *(u fill in the blanks)* and not souls.
4. Do you believe the pastor is as anointed as he was last year?
5. Have you noticed a lot of people are leaving?
6. I think our pastor travels too much, don't you?
7. I sure did like the pastor and his wife better when our ministry was smaller, didn't you?
8. Do you think the church services are too long?
9. I sure wish pastor wouldn't preach so hard?
10. Don't you believe the pastor makes too much money?
11. The pastor always seems to be focused on the offering more than the word of God.
12. Does the pastor's wife seem unfriendly to you?
13. Does the pastor shake your hand after church?
14. I don't like the songs we sing, do you?
15. There's too much emphasis on (you fill in the blank) and not enough on the word...
16. Everyone is saying... many people said this or that. *The truth is no one said anything.*

17. Don't you believe that the pastor's kids should be more spiritual than they are?
18. Can you believe that the pastor's kids sin?

STAGE SIX: THE DECEPTION STAGE

Here's where these people begin to be unchangeable. They are caught up in their own lie and believe it to be truth.

"This I say, therefore, and testify in the Lord, that you should no longer walk as the rest of the Gentiles walk, in the futility of their mind, having their understanding darkened, being alienated from the life of God, because of the ignorance that is in them, because of the blindness of their heart; who, being past feeling, have given themselves over to lewdness, to work all uncleanness with greediness." Ephesians 4:17-19 NKJV

I had a couple leave my church after being connected with me for at least five years. They didn't come and see me, or sit down with me to discuss how they were feeling. I sensed in my spirit for months that they were not acting right. I would ask them over and over again if there was anything wrong. They always answered with, *"No, we love you and the church."*

One day I got an email from them. After five years of pouring into them and praying for their success, this is what they said to me.

"Bishop we believe that God is done with us at The Favor Center. God has called us to be soul winners, and we feel that you are putting too much focus on television and not evangelism... God has led us to move on..."

That's it! Can you believe it? First of all, this couple did not bring one person to my church through evangelism in five years, they couldn't show you one person they led to the Lord or one life they had helped change. However, we receive letter after letter from people who have been touched, saved, helped and delivered through the television ministry.

Let me tell you where the Lord *supposedly* led them. They are now attending some home group on Sundays. They leave their living room to sit at someone's kitchen table. They call that *'God leading them.'* They left a house where there is awesome praise and worship offered up, preaching that will challenge and change you and a group of people who will help you grow and succeed. All to sit in someone's house who is not sanctioned nor called by God to lead them. Let me be clear this is **not** the leading of the Holy Spirit.

It is at this stage where they begin to become so convinced of their lies that they are self-vindicated. No one can reach them now. Not only are these people deceiving others, they are now deceiving themselves.

STAGE SEVEN: THE OPEN REBELLION STAGE

At this stage they are no longer hiding. They come right out in the open to fight you. They have built such a confidence in their own deception and lies that they feel justified in attacking the pulpit with all their might and hatred. I've said it once, and I will say it again. You haven't seen a good fight until you see a church fight.

STAGE EIGHT: EXECUTION STAGE

This stage goes along with stage seven... the spirit of rebellion creates the execution stage; how to rise up and attack the headship. Remember, rebellion is as the sin of witchcraft.

We must stand up and fight these insurrectionists before they reach stage six, seven and eight. There's hope for change if we can reach them, or expose them before the last three stages. Once they reach this level of rebellion, God sees them as witches and devil worshippers. Exodus 22:18 says. *"Thou shall not suffer a witch to live!"* God wants this spirit destroyed.

This open rebellion against our headship is satanic. It is not of God. God would never rise up against those that He has placed in authority.

"For there is no authority except from God, and the authorities that exist are appointed by God. Therefore whoever resists the authority resists the ordinance of God and those who resist will bring judgment on themselves. For rulers are not a terror to good works, but to evil. Do you want to be unafraid of the authority? Do what is good, and you will have praise from the same. For he is God's minister to you for good. But if you do evil, be afraid; for he does not bear the sword in vain; for he is God's minister, an avenger to execute wrath on him who practices evil. Therefore you must be subject, not only because of wrath but also for conscience' sake. For because of this you also pay taxes, for they are God's ministers attending continually to this very thing." Romans 13:1-7 NKJV

We must submit to delegated authority. The church is not a democracy, nor does the democracy way of thinking work in the church. The mind-set of the church must be the Kingdom mind-set. We must understand that Jesus is the King of the Kingdom we call church. Whoever the king places in authority now speaks and leads for the King. When you attack the leader you are actually attacking the King.

Even Michael the Archangel wouldn't rise up against God's delegated authority.

"Likewise also these dreamers defile the flesh, reject authority, and speak evil of dignitaries. Yet Michael the archangel, in contending with the devil, when he disputed about the body of Moses, dared not bring against him a reviling accusation, but said, "The Lord rebuke you!" But these speak evil of whatever they do not know; and whatever they know naturally, like brute beasts, in these things they corrupt themselves. Woe to them! For they have gone in the way of Cain, have run greedily in the error of Balaam for profit, and perished in the rebellion of Korah." Jude 8-11 NKJV

Did you see what the Lord said through His word? These dreamers defile the flesh, reject authority; they speak out against leaders and those in greatness. There is a fine line between the Freedom of Speech and the freedom to say what you want to damage and hurt those in leadership. That is wrong! Words are sharp weapons. Words can create wounds in someone that could take years to heal.

In America, we have gotten out of hand on how we allow people to talk and speak about our president and those in positions of authority. I don't care if they are republican, democrat or independent. We have no right to say the things we say.

In my opinion, I believe the reason the world has become so negative and speaking wrong about leadership is because we have digressed in the church and how we treat God's leaders. As the church goes, so goes the world. When the church stops respecting God's leaders expect the world around the church to grow worse.

This stage is where the person is now so deceived they are convinced they are operating in the spirit of the Lord. However, they are not. I assure you that they have been totally deceived. They are now what I believe to be unreachable... not capable of being mentored. There are many who will be deceived in that day and say, *"Lord, Lord,"* but you know that Jesus warned us that He doesn't know such people.

WOLVES IN SHEEP CLOTHING

If Lucifer or any of his demons entered the church, and said they were there to take it over and throw the headship out, most of us would rise up, rebuke the enemy and cast him and his hordes out of the church and our local body. Think for a moment, none of us want to see the enemy ruin our church or our pastors. However, week after week across this country that's exactly what happens. Boards rise up, people rise up and staff rise up against the man or woman of God to cast them down and throw them out.

I have seen some terrible church fights in my time, and each one was done in the name of the Lord. I've watched men face off with the man of God with the intention of fighting him. These are supposed to be spirit-filled and anointed men who are there to lift up and support the pulpit, not destroy it. However, many of us have been witnesses to such atrocities.

"Beware of false prophets, who come to you in sheep's clothing, but inwardly they are ravenous wolves. You will know them by their fruits." Matthew 7:15-16 NKJV

Wolves travel in packs; they never hang out alone. Wolves always send a wolf out to work their way into the flock of sheep. They crawl under the skin of a fallen sheep in order to get close to the flock. No flock would ever allow a wolf to enter intentionally so how does this happen? The flock is so caught up in feeding and grazing in the pasture that they lose focus on what's going on around them. What appears to be like them is not what they believe to be true. The sheep closest to them is really a wolf getting close to do harm to it.

When the wolf disguised as a sheep gets close enough, it will bite one of the sheep's hind legs to cripple its walk. Now, after trusting the wrong sheep, which was really a wolf, the once healthy sheep that had a great life and a great walk, has been weakened.

Now, when the shepherd begins to lead the flock on to the next pasture, or season, the wounded sheep has a problem keeping up with the flock. The flock begins to get further and further away. Once it is alone, the wolf pack appears and devours it for food.

This same pattern is how the enemy deceives and robs our churches. Satan knows you would never allow him in the flock so he sends a person (wolf) to get close to you.

"For I know this, that after my departure savage wolves will

come in among you, not sparing the flock. Also from among yourselves men will rise up, speaking perverse things, to draw away the disciples after themselves. Therefore watch, and remember that for three years I did not cease to warn everyone night and day with tears." Acts 20:29-31 NKJV

There has to be an attitude of attack against such people. There is no room to allow these kinds of people to stay close to the sheep who are trying to grow... trying to change... trying to fit in. The job of the shepherd is to sit watch over the sheep night and day. The shepherd makes sure the sheep are grazing safely and fellowshipping without confusion and strife so they can drink and eat for maturity. God never intended for us as leaders to allow these insurrectionists a place to ruin and control what God is trying to do through His headship.

What does the shepherd do? The shepherd stands watch. They are to guard and stay focused on the flock, not sit in the back and allow anything, or anyone, to enter to do physical harm against the people.

"Woe to the worthless shepherd, who leaves the flock! A sword shall be against his arm and against his right eye; His arm shall completely wither, and his right eye shall be totally blinded." Zechariah 11:17 NKJV

Document Your Thoughts

CHAPTER SEVEN

SIGNS OF DISLOYALTY

$\mathscr{D}$isloyalty is a secret weapon used by your enemies to destroy you from within. The goal of the enemy is to find someone in your organization that has become disgruntled by your leadership. Remember, it will be those you have chosen to lead for you. They will rise up behind your back, or the backs of other leaders, and begin to build a following of angry, dissatisfied people.

Sometimes this can turn into the most hideous of battles. I've seen some battles between leaders and headship in my lifetime that made me sick to my stomach. It is ridiculous to think that these people who rise up against the senior pastor believe they are led by the Spirit of God.

Disloyalty doesn't happen overnight. It takes time for someone to rise up and begin to destroy leadership with their words.

40 SIGNS OF DISLOYALTY

1. ***Moral weaknesses you can not correct...*** Those who begin to struggle with moral issues usually try to hide it for as long as they can. This sin will eventually show up in the mask of being overly holy. I've witnessed many that became overly holy and overly critical of those in moral struggles when they began to break down in their moral purity. The key to this sign is that you can't correct them. They won't have it. You are not allowed to even question them on the subject. The clue to their guilt will be their anger. As a matter of fact, most of those who are guilty will become angry when questioned. Anger is a clue of guilt.

2. ***Poor Financial Habits...*** God doesn't give us money. Nowhere in the Bible does it declare that God gave anyone money. Laws decide financial increase. When someone is revealing bad financial habits they are a prime candidate to

become disloyal. If they can't do right with their finances they won't do right with those you place under them. Money most always reveals character flaws in people. If God decided where money went then why does the mafia have it and the missionary doesn't? Money is decided by the laws you obey, and the lack of money is decided by the laws you have disobeyed. God runs the universe by His laws.

3. ***Those who think they know more than the leader and think they can lead better...*** There are many who are smarter than I am. However, when those under me start believing that I can't teach them, or lead them, they will begin to break connection with me and start trying to connect others to themselves. Their attitude in meetings will show; always wanting to add something to what you are mentoring. Trust me. You must silence them immediately. You're the door to those who are connected to you.

4. ***The wounded who have never recovered from their hurts...*** Wounded people leak issues. Many come into our churches, or leadership, who have not healed from their last place of leadership or ministry. They won't allow others to correct them. I've had people come from other churches that were severely wounded. They served in leadership at their last church, and through sad events the church they served folded and the leader left. The pastor left those who were connected to him in disarray. When those leaders came over to me they were not ready to be placed in leadership. They needed to time to heal. I placed a few of them immediately in leadership, and it ended up costing me dearly. Work with those who are wounded through their ministry hurts. They have to forgive and let it go.

5. ***Those who are not willing to be trained or retrained...*** They use words like *"I know... I know. "I've been in ministry for years..."* Those who come to your

meetings should always bring a notepad, ready to listen and glean. If they don't they are not interested in what you know, but in what you have.

6. ***Those who always have to let others know their credentials...*** I had a person on staff for years that would always have to let those around them know what they had done, what titles they had and what accomplishments they had made. At first, I thought they were just proud of what they had done. In the end, they had a hidden agenda. Eventually they left my ministry and started their own.

7. ***Those who refuse to do menial jobs around the church or business...*** Always watch out for people who say that's not my job description. Sometimes I will leave trash sitting around in certain areas and watch to see which one of those connected to me pick it up. Those who step over the trash may have a problem with serving others.

8. ***Someone who is constantly at war with their spouse...*** Marriage takes commitment. Marriage is the breeding ground where loyalty and commitment are proven. When married couples in your leadership are always fighting, watch out, this can be a sure sign that they will turn on you.

9. ***Those who get irritated and have wrong reactions when you correct them...*** Correction decides connection. The quality of a leader will be in proportion to their ability to take correction. If those under you will not allow you to correct them, move swiftly away from them and prepare to remove them from leadership. Watch out for those who are easily offended. The heart of offense can become a heart that is bitter and poisoned.

10. ***Someone who always gives excuses and justifies***

themselves in an error.

11. **A person who does not keep their promises...** Do a credit check on those you bring around you in leadership. If their credit score is terrible that could be a clue that they are not good at keeping their promises. Of course, this is not always the case. Discover the reason before you judge. Do background checks on everyone who is connecting with you to help build your business or ministry.

12. **A person who is always lobbying for promotion and recognition...** These kinds of people live life with a false expectation on how you should be treating them. They are consistently waiting for compliments and recognition over the smallest things they do. If someone thinks they are serving you, but you pay them, watch yourself. They are not really serving if you are paying them. Their high expectation for compliments and recognition could be a severe sign they have a wound of rejection or insecurities. They will become a well of disappointment, not just for you, but disappointment in themselves. When false expectation or overly high expectation is placed on someone, the result is usually a season of disappointment. Deferred hope makes a heart sick and causes the mind to become critical.

13. **Someone who has never been criticized or corrected... amateur leaders... young leaders...** This is not to say that young leaders can't lead... It is to say that they are easily distracted. One reason is that they haven't really learned the mind-set of loyalty. Take time to train young leaders.

14. **Someone who is not attentive and taking notes, or uninvolved while teaching and preaching...** Those who are connected to you will want to hear what you have to say. Any leader who sits under your teaching but appears to

be disinterested is going to be a problem down the road. This attitude is a sure clue that something is wrong in them. They may have picked up an offense, listened to someone talk about you or talked about you themselves. Now, they don't want to learn from you.

15. **Someone who's not faithful in helping other ministries succeed...** Look for non-team-players. They are going to be a prime candidate for insurrection. I want those around me concerned for all areas of the church, not just theirs.

16. **Someone who does not tithe or sow consistently into your ministry or life...** I could write pages on this one sign. People will never be loyal to any place they won't put their money in. Tithe is a no-brainer. If someone in your leadership doesn't tithe, immediately correct them. If they still will not tithe after correction, immediately sit them down. Those who won't tithe are under a curse. They are suppose to be broke... they are suppose to be sick... they are walking and living under a curse. Anyone around them and connected to them are under their curse.

17. **Someone who does not attend your meetings regularly...** I hate inconsistency. I understand as a head leader that sometimes meetings and gatherings have to be missed because of work, sickness or because someone is out of town. I watch for the person's inconsistency in attendance. Especially at special events or meetings. I watch their attendance to the midweek service. I listen for their reasons why they weren't in attendance. I have witnessed in my own ministry the disloyal spirit that came from those who wanted to be a leader, but wouldn't make the meetings as others were asked to do.

18. **Someone who approves of someone who makes wrong decisions...** Here's another one that gets my blood boiling. Wrong decisions are supposed to create seasons of wrong consequences. This is how we learn through experience. When someone consistently steps in to help those you are allowing life to train, then they are being counterproductive. They are hindering your leadership. We become an enemy to God when we bail out those God is teaching through consequence.

19. **Someone who poisons or tries to poison your thinking about others...** This one doesn't need much commentary. It's self explanatory. If you allow a serpent to hang out in your leadership, expect everyone to eventually be bitten and poisoned. These people will not sit silent; they will spew their poison on all who will listen. They are those who won't shut up. Trust me. The only way to deal with a snake is to kill it. By killing it I mean by sitting it down or asking it to leave.

20. **A person who will not mingle and interact with others...** Loners have a problem. Either with themselves or those around them. Those who never mingle and interact with the group usually have internal damage. That damage will eventually leak. Demand your leaders to mingle; to grow your ministry.

21. **A person who has a controlling spouse...** How a person deals with their spouse will be a pure reflection on how they will deal with others. If a married person can't stand up against their spouse when their spouse is wrong, or out of order, they will most likely never stand up for you when the times of decision come.

   I have a pastor friend who asked his board members not to hang out or sit and counsel with a certain person who left the ministry in the wrong way. This person left with hatred and went around discrediting the church and its senior pastor. When the pastor had finished asking for the board not to mingle with this person, one board members' wife spoke up and said, *"You're asking me to disobey the Lord. The Lord has directed me to counsel this person."* This is so ridiculous. First of all, God would not ask you to do something without the direction of your headship. This woman was very controlling and couldn't stand to be told what to do. When I was approached as their bishop, I told the senior pastor that she was out of order and if she didn't want to line up then let the line out. That's exactly what happened, they left. Good! Now, we can get on with unity and church business.

22. **A person who always shifts the blame on others...** Someone who can't take correction is one thing, but a person who always says their failure is the fault of someone else really has a problem. When someone shifts the blame they are usually not teachable. The wound of rejection keeps them from facing their mistakes to fix them.

23. **Someone who thinks the senior pastor makes too much money...** If you have someone who believes like this sow my book into their life, **"7 Strategic Prayers You Should Pray Over Your Pastor."**

24. **A person who is not a team player...** Team players are important, and there is no room in your leadership for individuality.

25. **Someone who is comfortable in your enemy's presence...** If you're comfortable in my enemy's presence, then you are probably in agreement to my enemy's opinion about me. I have a problem with those who call themselves my friend, or leader but can sit in the presence of those who are attacking me and talking about the church. When asked

about it they tell me, *"Well I'm just being Christ like."* The truth is that you are being disloyal.

26. **Someone who never picks a side...** This goes along with number twenty-five. I had a staff person who would never really pick a side no matter what happened. You are either on my side or you're not. We can't be divided in times of war. A house that is divided will fall. I found out that people would come to them and complain about me and my vision. Instead of defending me, they would just tell these people to pray. One time, a secretary questioned this staff person about some money transactions. She wanted to know why the deposit was different than what was counted. When asked this question, my administrator shrugged their shoulders as if to say, *"Well, I don't know,"* instead of letting her know what we were doing with the money. This gave the impression to the secretary that I was taking the money out of the offering bag. I'm telling you right now... fire anyone who doesn't pick your side, or a side.

27. **A person who acts super-spiritual...** Come on, you know all about these kinds of people. Everything is supernatural... Everything is spiritual... Give me a break!

28. **Someone who says they always have a word from God...** God went silent for four hundred years after the book of Malachi; however, now He can't seem to stop talking. Those who always have a word from God have only gotten a word from their own head. God will speak to the headship first about the house and His direction for the church before He speaks to any leader.

29. **A person who is comfortable in the presence of the ungodly...** God called us to save the ungodly and to witness to them; not hang out with them. I don't understand what light has in common with darkness. Someone who is

comfortable around the ungodly probably hasn't made their mind up on how to commit to the things of God. They have yet to choose a side. (Reference #26)

30. **Someone who trivializes what you feel is important.**

31. **Someone who believes you owe them something...** These people will walk in resentment toward the leader. No matter what you do, you owe them. No matter what they do, you owe them.

32. **A person who complains about others to you will complain about you in your absence...** People are always complaining... complaining about you as their leader. These kinds of people never see what they are doing; only what others aren't doing. Be cautious about allowing a complainer to hang out with you. God despises complainers.

33. **Someone who is silent in an argument. They won't speak up and let their vote be counted...** I had a board member who would never speak up in our meetings no matter what we were discussing. They would just sit there. For the longest time I took their silence as agreement. No, not true. Those who are in agreement with you will always speak up.

34. **A person who will not follow your instruction...** Delayed obedience is disobedience. God doesn't bless anything that is in disobedience.

35. **A person with a hidden agenda...** No matter how hard someone serves you, if they have a hidden agenda they will eventually leave you. They will usually leave in a wrong way. People who are godly servants serve because that's what they are; God's servants. If someone is serving with a hidden

agenda they are not sent by God. They were sent by ambition. These people are about one thing and one thing only... their agenda and their promotion.

36. ***Someone who is always over flirtatious...*** This is for men. Watch out for flirtatious women. There is no room for this in the Kingdom. The end result will create disloyalty in the heart of the leader towards his wife and family. I believe that Satan sends these kinds of women in our churches to distract the man of God. I don't care what kind of problems you are having at home; never share it with others, especially with those of the opposite sex. Bonds are created when problems are shared.

37. ***A person who causes you frustration during and after great attacks...*** Those who cannot discern you've just come out of a season of attack are more concerned about their needs than the needs of the leader. Be very careful with those around you who cause you frustration. Frustration can create seasons of wrong decisions. These people will not stick with you when the waters in your ministry or business start getting rough. Frustration is a distraction. Frustration weakens your focus and robs your faith.

38. ***Those who are jealous over someone else's promotions...*** Jealousy is the offspring of bitterness. First of all, those who are jealous don't believe in themselves. Secondly, they are wounded and focused on others and what they have instead of what they could be.

39. ***Someone who will not praise and worship during service...*** I've seen this over and over again. In the beginning of my ministry, there were leaders that would sit in service and never worship... never praise... never lift their hands. I would ask them why? They would always have some lame excuse. One person in particular, would cross their

arms the minute the praise and worship minister would instruct the congregation to lift their hands. I asked them why? They answered with, *"**No man is going to tell me what to do...**"*

40. ***A person who is consistently depressed and has no joy...*** Those who stay depressed are hard to reach. Those who are hard to reach will eventually become lost in the movement of the organization.

I know it seems there is a lot to watch out for. Trust me, it will be worth your time and effort to learn and teach these signs. Let me be clear. Just because someone is showing signs of disloyalty doesn't mean they can't be ministered to and fixed.

The mistake is made when the headship ignores what needs to be addressed. Ignoring these signs may prove to be fatal for you and your ministry or business. Don't ignore them; address them... teach about them. Teach those around you to expose anyone who is showing these signs and symptoms of disloyalty. Let's work together to clean up God's house.

CHAPTER EIGHT

WHY YOU NEED A PASTOR

"*And I will give you shepherds according to my heart, who will feed you with knowledge and understanding. "Then it shall come to pass, when you are multiplied and increased in the land in those days," says the Lord, "that they will say no more, 'The ark of the covenant of the Lord.' It shall not come to mind, nor shall they remember it, nor shall they visit it, nor shall it be made anymore. "At that time Jerusalem shall be called The Throne of the Lord, and all the nations shall be gathered to it, to the name of the Lord, to Jerusalem. No more shall they follow the dictates of their evil hearts." Jeremiah 3:15-17 NKJV*

WHY WE NEED A PASTOR

God said the day was coming when there would be no need for the Ark of the Covenant. He was going to provide shepherds.

The pastor is the replacement for the Ark of God. God uses the pastor to send on the battle field.

You must understand some key things about the Ark of the Covenant to fully understand the power and importance of the pastor.

The Ark was the place where God housed His presence and power. In this presence, His power would be hidden. The Ark was made of acacia wood and covered in pure gold inside and out so if you cut the Ark down the middle and opened it you would see gold...wood... gold.

Gold represents the Godhead and wood represents humanity. Acacia wood is the hardest wood known to man. Acacia wood will not rot. Acacia wood is a type of Christ in that, when Christ died, corruption could not touch him.

The gold, wood and gold also represented that Jesus, the Messiah, would come from deity, enter humanity and then return back to deity. We know that the Ark of the Covenant was a type of Christ in the Old Testament. However, in Jeremiah, God said that we would no longer ask for the Ark. God has now placed that assignment on the man or woman of God. It is the pastor who now sits on the high place. This is why there is a platform in church. It isn't a stage for entertainment. The platform is the high place where the pastor, a type of the Ark, can sit above the people and protect them from the wolves that try to sneak unaware. The enemy comes in to steal, kill and destroy those who are deceived. The pastor is the Ark prepared for battle.

CONTENT OF THE ARK

*"Then indeed, even the first covenant had ordinances of divine service and the earthly sanctuary. For a tabernacle was prepared: the first part, in which was the lamp stand, the table, and the showbread, which is called the sanctuary; and behind the second veil, the part of the tabernacle which is called the Holiest of All, which had the golden censer and the ark of the covenant overlaid on all sides with gold, **in which were the golden pot that had the manna, Aaron's rod that budded, and the tablets of the covenant; and above it were the cherubim of glory overshadowing the mercy seat." Hebrews 9:1-5 NKJV***

Above the Ark were two cherubim angels whose wings touched each other. They were the covering and shadowing of the Ark. There were tree types of angels in heaven...

1. Arch Angels: Principalities, protectors of nations. We already discussed this group in the first part of the book
2. Seraphim: They stand above the Lord singing, Holy, Holy, Holy is the Lord. They are the guardians of God's atmosphere.
3. Cherubim: They denote the power of knowing and beholding God. They are filled with divine wisdom. Wisdom is poured out through them. God promised to commune with Moses, "From

between the Cherubim." (Genesis 25:22)

We see the shadow of the Spirit of Wisdom over the pastor. These Cherubim are the fountain, or covering, of God's protection and here is where the wisdom of God communes to the Pastor, "between the Cherubim." Cherubim covered the mercy seat as well. God's mercy is strongest when we are connected to those God has placed over us. Satan knows that disconnecting from the man of God can create seasons of loss and pain.

INSIDE THE ARK

1. *Golden pot of manna*
2. *Aaron's rod that budded*
3. *The broken tablets of the covenant*

In the senior pastor is the mantle, the message and the miracle. You can't have these qualities without the senior pastor. There has to be a covenant, a connection to the man of God.

THE MANTLE

The mantle is the calling, the holy selection that comes on the man of God. The mantle is the manna, the breath of God placed in the mouth of the pastor. When we come to the church we are sitting in the place where God has placed His manna in the mouth of the man of God. God wants to rain down over the gathering of people and have that manna, which is God's word, stick on those who hear.

There was a process to the manna. The manna was the second thing released on the earth. The dew would fall first and cover the earth. Then after the dew was in place, manna would fall and stick to the ground for the children of Israel to eat. "*And when the dew fell on the camp in the night, the manna fell on it" Numbers 11:9 NKJV.* The earth represents the flesh, the dew represents the Spirit of God, and the manna represents God's spoken word. So the first thing we must understand is that unless the dew covers the ground, the Word of God (manna) will not stick or be able to sustain.

The children of Israel survived for forty years in a wilderness that would have killed others because they ate the manna. Their shoes never wore out, their clothes never wore out and their bodies never became sick. Their things were protected and lasted through the consuming of the manna.

The dew, or the Spirit of God, must first be applied on the ground... the flesh. The Spirit of God falls when we praise and worship. God inhabits our praise. ***"But thou art holy, O thou that inhabits the praises of Israel." Psalm 22:3.*** He sends the Spirit to hover over us and in us. God's presence is the only place where our weaknesses will die. Every time we gather for worship service I watch for people who just sit there and don't worship. They just look around as if those who are participating are bothering them. Most of the time, these people never receive the word that is preached. The manna can't attach to the ground, or flesh, because these people have not been wet with the dew of God's Spirit. If you are ignoring this process expect everything in your life to break down and wear out. Your marriage, your mind, your health, your job, your finances - they are all attached to the receiving and eating of the manna. No worship, no rain... no rain (dew), no manna.

THE MESSAGE

*"For since, in the wisdom of God, the world through wisdom did not know God, it pleased God through the foolishness of **the message** preached to save those who believe." 1 Corinthians 1:21-22 NKJV*

*"But the Lord stood with me and strengthened me, so **that the message might be preached** fully through me, and that all*

the Gentiles might hear. Also I was delivered out of the mouth of the lion. And the Lord will deliver me from every evil work and preserve me for His heavenly kingdom. To Him be glory forever and ever. Amen!" 2 Timothy 4:17-18 NKJV

The broken tablets represent the power of the message of God. God's laws are hidden in the man of God. They are in broken pieces only to be placed in whole when they are delivered to the body of Christ.

God imparts His wisdom for change through the man of God. The pastor is the voice of conviction... the voice of empowerment... the voice of love. His voice and message carries power to change cities and nations. The battle can only be won when there is a body of believers who under gird him and lift his hands.

"How then shall they call on Him in whom they have not believed? And how shall they believe in Him of whom they have not heard? And how shall they hear without a preacher? And how shall they preach unless they are sent?" Romans 10:14-15 NKJV

The pastor is the person in your life who carries the instruction to preach so others can hear and be changed. Present seasons might become permanent if we do not understand that without the shepherd in our lives we may live life void of the instruction that could change us.

God has always used men and called them to be His deliverer in word and deed. I would be very careful touching, attacking or even talking about those whom God has chosen in His holy selection to be His messenger.

THE MIRACLE

In the man of God is the power of a miracle. I believe when the person God has selected for governmental order is in position, the atmosphere is pregnant with the budding rod of Aaron. Let's discuss this spiritual phenomenon. The rod of Aaron was cut off of the root of the tree. In all perspectives, the rod was a dead piece of wood. It lost its power to reproduce, grow and change every year when it was cut off from the whole.

However, Aaron's rod would bud every year. It would show signs of new life every year. This is completely out of the norm. The rod was dead; it had no root system to reproduce. That's the miracle of the pastor. When you allow the pastor to be in his position over you and your family, you are allowing the miracle of new growth and change to take place.

The enemy would flee when the Ark came down to the battlefield. The pastor is the ark for battle over the enemy in your life that keeps trying to defeat and beat you down.

"So it was whenever the ark set out, that Moses said: "Rise up, O Lord! Let Your enemies be scattered, And let those who hate You flee before You." Numbers 10:35 NKJV

"But they presumed to go up to the mountaintop. Nevertheless, neither the ark of the covenant of the Lord nor Moses departed from the camp. Then the Amalekites and the Canaanites who dwelt in that mountain came down and attacked them, and drove them back as far as Hormah." Numbers 14:44-45 NKJV

The attitude of the people over the ark put fear in the hearts of their enemies. I believe the same is true about the pastor. When the body has a strong affection and loyalty to the pastor, their praise and shouts will show forth. The enemy will fear and tremble when this happens. The enemy would usually leave when the Ark was on the battlefield. The enemy feared the power of God that was placed in the Ark. The people of God had a sense of praise and joy when the Ark was with them and heading towards their enemy. This is true with the pastor. The enemy fears the result of battle when he sees the connection between the people the pastor.

When the children of Israel had sinned the Ark wouldn't show up on the field of battle. The guilt of sin stopped the movement of the Ark. The result was loss every time. The same is true in our churches. When the people stop living right and stop respecting the pastor because of rejection or offense, the people stop bringing the pastor to the battlefield. The result is the same, LOSS! Loss of land... Loss of finances... Loss of friends and family... and in some cases... loss of life.

"And when the ark of the covenant of the Lord came into the camp, all Israel shouted so loudly that the earth shook. Now when the Philistines heard the noise of the shout, they said, "What does the sound of this great shout in the camp of the Hebrews mean?" Then they understood that the ark of the Lord had come into the camp. So the Philistines were afraid, for they said, "God has come into the camp!" And they said, "Woe to us!" 1 Samuel 4:5-7 NKJV

Many people believe that the pastor is someone the deacons hired to motivate and encourage a church. They think he is nothing more than a hireling on their payroll, and if they don't like what he stands for they can just take a vote and fire him.

I've seen many pastors' families ruined because of how they were treated by their so-called bosses. I've witnessed some of the meanest and cruelest things that can be done against God's man. I wouldn't want to be some people on judgment day. There are those in our churches who have stored up a heavy wrath from God because of how they've treated and talked about God's man.

No one has the right to correct or think they are the boss over a pastor. No deacon board or church board has been given such authority. The government of the house comes from and through the senior pastor. I had a good friend tell me that the government of God will always produce the glory of God. The glory of God will always create the gold in the house. Money and increase are attached to our reaction to the man of god.

Death comes to those who wrongly touch the Ark.
Look at the story below. When Uzzah reached out and put his
hand on the Ark the anger of the Lord was aroused, and Uzzah
was punished. So will all those be punished who reach out and
lay hold of the man of God; whether by words or deeds.

*"And when they came to Nachon's threshing floor, Uzzah put
out his hand to the ark of God and took hold of it, for the oxen
stumbled. Then the anger of the Lord was aroused against
Uzzah, and God struck him there for his error; and he died
there by the ark of God. And David became angry because of
the Lord's outbreak against Uzzah; and he called the name of
the place Perez Uzzah to this day. David was afraid of the
Lord that day; and he said, "How can the ark of the Lord come
to me?" So David would not move the ark of the Lord with him
into the City of David; but David took it aside into the house of
Obed-Edom the Gittite. The ark of the Lord remained in the
house of Obed-Edom the Gittite three months. And the Lord
blessed Obed-Edom and all his household."* 2 Samuel 6:1-11
NKJV

Aaron's rod would bud supernaturally. It would produce
disconnected from what was, because of what it had now been
connected to. The pastor is the source for miracles. Maybe you
had to walk away from friends or family members to stay
connected to your local church and pastor. Don't be
discouraged. God is going to have you budding even though you
had to walk away from what was. Your connection to what is will
produce incredible miracles. Stay connected no matter what.

When we stay connected to the pastor we activate the
mercy seat over us. I believe there are four different types of
followers.

1. ***The passive follower:*** They only reach when it is
   convenient, or when their personal efforts do not produce

their desired result. They subconsciously expect the pastor and the church to produce success for them.

2. **The parasite follower**: They pursue for credibility, not for correction. They will use the name and influence of a church, or pastor, to manipulate others into a relationship. They want what the pastor has earned, not what he has learned. They want reputation without preparation.

3. **The prodigal follower**: They enter and exit the relationship freely. When serious correction occurs, they move toward another pastor, or another church who does not know them and their flaws. They distance themselves when the pastor, or the church, encounters personal attacks, difficulties, loss of credibility, false accusation or persecution. They only return when their pigpen becomes unbearable.

4. **The productive follower**: They have a servant's heart. They never make a major decision without the counsel and feedback of their pastor. They view their pastor and church as a dominant gift from God. They love their pastor as much as themselves. These followers view their connection as a divine privilege by God.

TEN SIGNS OF A PRODUCTIVE FOLLOWER

1. *The productive follower will invest everything to stay in the presence of their pastor and church.*
2. *The productive follower follows the counsel of the pastor.*
3. *The productive follower reveals the secrets and dreams of his heart with the pastor and the church.*
4. *The productive follower freely discusses his mistakes and pain with the pastor.*
5. *The productive follower defines clearly his*

expectations to the pastor.

6. *The productive follower gladly sows seeds of appreciation back into the life of their pastor.*

7. *The productive follower ultimately receives the mantle of the pastor he serves.*

8. *The productive follower moves toward the shelter of the pastor during a season of great attack and warfare.*

9. *The productive follower will change his own schedule to invest time in the presence of their pastor.*

10. *The productive follower is someone who discerns, respects and pursues the answers God has stored in the pastor for their life.* [iii]

Document Your Thoughts

Closing Thoughts

I want to make it clear, this is a study to teach the body of Christ how to recognize and deal with people who are sent by the enemy to divide us and ultimately destroy what God is building in someone else. This is not a manual for a "witch hunt;" trying to hang and burn those who are just different.

Be mature... Be a Christian... Walk in love. This will help the axe of leadership to be received better. We must all stand against the false prophets, those who are not able to be trained, those who don't want to be taught and those who fight change. Let me caution you, not everyone who fights change or doesn't want to change is possessed with the spirit of disloyalty. More than likely, they are just scared. They lack one necessary ingredient to make them better... **courage!**

- *IT TAKES COURAGE TO CHANGE.*
- *IT TAKES COURAGE TO ADMIT YOU NEED CHANGE.*
- *IT TAKES COURAGE TO TRY SOMETHING DIFFERENT.*
- *IT TAKES COURAGE TO BE CORRECTED AND CHOOSE TO STAY CONNECTED.*

The reason so many sit in our churches the same year after year is because they lack the courage to change. For someone to change they first have to recognize they are in need of something more. Their marriage needs more... their finances need more... they need more. Change is the answer for us to have and do more. Change is the ingredient that makes us better. It takes courage to stand up after reading this book and realize that we all, at one time, have probably been used as a disloyal insurrectionist.

I know this is hard to swallow, but it's true. We all have talked about leaders and pastors if we are honest. We have even sat and listened while others were talking and being destructive in their actions to what another was trying to build.

Just because we sat in wrong places or talked about leadership at some point in our lives doesn't make us an insurrectionist. It is those who continue to talk and be full of bitterness and anger that are turning their hearts hard to correction and change; setting themselves up to be used by the enemy.

Never allow your mind to wander so far that it stops you from sitting down with your leaders and talking to them about what's hurting or troubling you.

No one can stay in one place forever. If you sense your time is up in the house you've been serving, approach the Lord first. Then, go straight to your pastor and let him know. Here's a word to the wise. If God is done with you in one place, He will already be opening the door for the next place. God will never send you down the ladder, but always up for mentorship and training.

Allow the man of God over you to create a proper exodus for you. Being "sent" is more powerful than just "went." Never leave hurt. Never leave mad. Make sure that you are really being sent by the Lord instead of being stirred up by someone you know that is discontent. Disgruntled people always try to persuade others to feel what they're feeling. Misery loves company.

It is my prayer that this book will help heal the people of God. I am confident that it will help slow down wrong people's influence and help keep unity in the local church.

Thanks for reading it. I love writing books. They have become my passion. You, the reader, have become my partner in this endeavor. You make it worthwhile for me to take the time to write.

Dr. G

Decision Page

May I Invite You to Make Jesus Christ the Lord of Your Life?

The Bible says, *"That if you will confess with your mouth the Lord Jesus, and will believe in your heart that God raised Him from the dead, you will be saved. For with the heart man believes unto righteousness; and with the mouth confession is made for salvation."* Romans 10:9-10

Pray this prayer with me today:
"Dear Jesus, I believe that You died for me and rose again on the third day. I confess to You that I am a sinner. I need Your love and forgiveness. Come into my life, forgive my sins and give me eternal life. I confess You now as my Lord. Thank You for my salvation! I walk in Your peace and joy from this day forward. Amen!"

Signed_____

Date _____

[Mail this in to Dr. Grillo]

☐ Yes, Dr. Jerry! I made a decision to accept Christ as my personal Savior today, and I would like to put on your mailing list.

Name_____

Address_____

City_____State _____ Zip_____

Phone_____ Email_____

Godstrong Ministries
P.O. Box 3707, Hickory N.C. 28603
828.325.4773 Fax: 828.325.4877 www.fogzone.net

If you would like to have Dr. Jerry Grillo speak at your next Conference, Business Meeting or host a Leadership Conference at your church contact:

Godstrong Ministries
P.O. Box 3707
Hickory, NC. 28601
Email us at FZM@charter.net
Call 1.888. FAVOR ME
1.888.328.6763

FOOTNOTE
[i] From Wikipedia, the free encyclopedia

[ii] Victory Life Church Website information. "Discerning the spirit of Absalom in the church.

[iii] Dr. Mike Murdock, The Law of Recognition, 1999, The Wisdom Center, 35-36.

Reaching Milli[...]

Partner With Dr. Jerry
As His Ministry Is Touc[...]
The World, Throug[...]
The Word Network[...]
Streaming Faith,
Fogzone Publishing [...]
GodStrong TV.

"...Peter called for his partners to be blessed with his overflo[...]
Luke

Church Meetings - Multitudes are ministered to in crusades and sem[...] throughout America in "The Favor Conferences." Bishop's heart is for the S[...] Pastors.

Books and Literature – Bishop has written over fourteen books... with ov[...] book ideas to be completed. "Daddy God" is given to many around the nati[...] a seed-book. Bishop's heart is to reach out to those in prisons an[...] accommodate those who are hurting; he sows "Daddy God" to a major[...] Prison Ministries around the nation.

Videos and Tapes – Thousands are listening to Bishop all over the cou[...] through his videos and tape ministry. He has over forty series to offer the Bo[...] Christ.

Television and Radio – The Favor message is being aired all over the nation. Bishop has app[...] on TBN, The Harvest Show, Daystar, Lesea Broadcasting, WBTV 49 Augusta GA., WATV 57 Atlan[...] and so many more

Watch Us
Live Online

WATCH FOR EVENTS AND CONFERENCES

GodStrongTV.com Online
Partnership
Donations
Bookstore
Video Archives
Monthly Book Special
About Us
Contact Us
Prayer Center

REAMING
AITH

Address [   ] Go   Need help?

LIVE BROADCAST

FOGZONE MINISTRIES   BOOKSTORE   MEDIA PAGE   PARTNER

hen You Log On To
ODSTRONGTV.COM

**Find Material To Promote You
To The Next Level In God**

Watch The Weekly Program

**Register For FREE Monthly
Newsletters And Gifts**

**Enjoy A Weekly Lesson With
Dr. Grillo's "Favor Minute"**

**Ask Questions and Dr. Grillo
Will Share His Insight**

**Visit Our Online Shop And Find
Dynamic Books, CD's, DVD's
and Videos at Discount Prices**

And Much, Much More....

WWW.GODSTRONGTV.COM

FOGZONE PUBLISHIN

GOD Has Given You a Message
Millions Are Waiting To Hear It!

Providing a number of quality services to meet your publishing needs.

* Proof Reading
* Formatting
* ISBN Number
* Barcode Services
* Copy Write
* Graphic Design

For More Information call 1 888 328 6763
or visit us online www.fogzonedesigns.com